Mindfulness Therapy

Day Rituals to Conquer Anxiety and Live in the Moment of Peace and Happiness Everyday

(Live in the Present Moment in Your Everyday Life)

Gregory Cota

Published by Rob Miles

© **Gregory Cota**

All Rights Reserved

Mindfulness Therapy: Day Rituals to Conquer Anxiety and Live in the Moment of Peace and Happiness Everyday (Live in the Present Moment in Your Everyday Life)

ISBN 978-1-989990-99-5

All rights reserved. No part of this guide may be reproduced in any form without permission in writing from the publisher except in the case of brief quotations embodied in critical articles or reviews.

Legal & Disclaimer

The information contained in this book is not designed to replace or take the place of any form of medicine or professional medical advice. The information in this book has been provided for educational and entertainment purposes only.

The information contained in this book has been compiled from sources deemed reliable, and it is accurate to the best of the Author's knowledge; however, the Author cannot guarantee its accuracy and validity and cannot be held liable for any errors or omissions. Changes are periodically made to this book. You must consult your doctor or get professional medical advice before using any of the suggested remedies, techniques, or information in this book.

Upon using the information contained in this book, you agree to hold harmless the Author from and against any damages, costs, and expenses, including any legal fees potentially resulting from the application of any of the information provided by this guide. This disclaimer applies to any damages or injury caused by the use and application, whether directly or indirectly, of any advice or information presented, whether for breach of contract, tort, negligence, personal injury, criminal intent, or under any other cause of action.

You agree to accept all risks of using the information presented inside this book. You need to consult a professional medical practitioner in order to ensure you are both able and healthy enough to participate in this program.

Table of Contents

INTRODUCTION 1

CHAPTER 1: THE POWER OF MEDITATION 4

CHAPTER 2: BREATHING CORRECTLY 10

CHAPTER 3: BREAKING FREE FROM NEGATIVITY 14

CHAPTER 4: THE GIFTS OF MINDFULNESS........................ 23

CHAPTER 5: REVITALIZING BENEFITS OF MINDFULNESS. WHO SHOULD PRACTICE IT? 39

CHAPTER 6: WHAT DO WE REALLY NEED IN LIFE? 47

CHAPTER 7: EIGHT MEDITATION TECHNIQUES FOR MINDFULNESS 57

CHAPTER 8: MOTIVATIONAL BOOKS AND SPEECHES 66

CHAPTER 9: WHO CAN BENEFIT FROM MINDFULNESS? ... 70

CHAPTER 10: HOW TO PRACTICE MINDFUL MEDITATION 75

CHAPTER 11: THE EVOLUTION OF SELF 81

CHAPTER 12: UNDERSTANDING STRESS AND ANXIETY AND HOW MINDFULNESS CAN RELIEVE THE TWO 87

CHAPTER 13: ESSENTIAL FOUNDATIONS OF YOUR PRACTICE.. 92

CHAPTER 14: MEDITATION TECHNIQUES 102

CHAPTER 15: THE 'HOW' OF MINDFULNESS 114

CHAPTER 16: WHY MEDITATE? 124

- CHAPTER 17: MEDITATION TECHNIQUE FOR BEGINNER 130
- CHAPTER 18: MEDITATION: THE MOST FUNDAMENTAL HABIT 134
- CHAPTER 19: GETTING STARTED – MINDFULNESS MEDITATION 141
- CHAPTER 20: BECOMING MORE CREATIVE 153
- CHAPTER 22: FOCUSED MEDITATION 161
- CHAPTER 23: MINDFULNESS FOR BEGINNERS: EVERYTHING YOU NEED TO KNOW.. 165
- CHAPTER 24: GROUP MINDFULNESS AND MORE TIPS ... 172
- CHAPTER 25: WHAT IS MINDFULNESS? 176
- CONCLUSION... 182

Introduction

Today more than ever, stress, depression and anxiety are as common as air pollution. This has caused many people to become sick with what's referred to as lifestyle or affluence diseases or sicknesses, which includes among others depression, anxiety, high cholesterol levels, obesity, cancers and heart disease. While it may look like society is progressing as a whole, the opposite seems to be true individually for many, especially in the areas of physical and emotional health.

While that may seem so much as bad news, there's also good news – there's something we can do to address it. Much of the things that go wrong in our lives are because of our inability to live purposefully. In other words, many of us live our lives on autopilot – void of any effort to steer the direction of how we want to truly live.

Purposeful living allows us to live our lives filled with great mental, emotional, and physical health. And while it may be said that to a great extent that society tends to greatly control or influence the way we live our lives, it's also true that we all have the ability to go against the grain – to change our lives for the best, not just better.

In this book, you'll know how to live life purposefully through the art of MINDFULNESS, which can help you win the war against mental, emotional and even physical health issues that come with today's "progressive" living society or your own personal circumstances. Particularly, you'll learn how to live mindfully in different ways: breathing, eating, visualizing and meditating. By the time you're done with this book, you'll be on your way to living the best life you can live, regardless of your personal circumstances and the very toxic world you may be living in. Peace in the midst of chaos – mindfulness living can give you that.

So if you're ready to start enjoying the best life you can ever live, turn the page and let's begin.

Chapter 1: The Power of Meditation

The reasons behind meditation have become somewhat lost over the years but thankfully, they are slowing beginning to break through once again. Many people believe that meditation is simply done to relax the mind, distress, and totally feel at peace. Although meditation does help with all these things, there is another reason why meditation is so important.

According to Abraham Hicks, we are not humans having a spiritual experience, we are spirits having a human experience and this is why meditation is so important because it is meditation that allows us to really feel this oneness.

What Meditation does for us

Meditation, after repeatedly practiced for a short time, opens up doors in the mind that we may not have known were even there. It strengthens the gateway of our consciousness and awakens us to see the world that is truly around us. What is common for someone who has started to meditate on a daily basis, is that their mind expands to more than just the physical planes but to the subconscious planes too, leaving this person totally awake in the world whilst most others are simply sleepwalking.

The idea of meditating can seem quite daunting to those who have never done it but it's a little like exercise in that the more you do it, the more strength you build and the more you begin to enjoy it. There are all different ways that we can get started with meditation and as you continue on with it, you'll find different times in the day that work best for you and your schedule. Some like to meditate upon awakening whereas others like to spring out of bed and get on with their day. Some like to unwind before sleep with an evening meditation whilst some like to turn the lights out and hit the pillow.

Morning Meditation

Morning meditation can be a great start to the day. Upon awakening, we have a choice whether that day will be a good day or a bad day. As we have just had a good nights sleep, when we wake we are rested and our mind will be the most peaceful it can be all day but some people wake up and start worrying about things that happened the day before or start panicking about what they must get done on that day and before you know it, that window to make it a great day has vanished.

Morning meditation can really help with this. Just 15 minutes can make all the difference. Upon waking, sit up in bed and keep your eyes closed. Focus on your breath as it is your base to stay grounded and quiet. If your mind wanders, always go back to the breath. Sit very still and just enjoy the stillness of the morning and allow your mind to remain still for as long as you can.

> Meditation is the journey
> from sound to silence,
> from movement to stillness,
> from a limited identity
> to unlimited space.
>
> Sri Ravi Shankar

Try Transcendenental Meditation

This method, also known as TM, is a wonderful method that everyone can have success with. The TM technique involves a mantra which a TM teacher would give you upon the arrival of your TM class. The idea of this technique is to literally tire out the brain. By repeating this mantra over and over again in your mind, you'll notice that after a while, this mantra becomes really tricky to keep repeating to yourself and this is when you stop saying it. Once you decide to stop saying it, you'll notice that your mind has become very still, very quiet, even as if you so in tune with your inner self that you feel the presence of your body as a separate entity. This is one of the easiest methods to try when it comes to getting into meditation.

Meditating in Nature

Nature is a beautiful place to find peace especially if you struggle to quiet the mind. The air is sweeter outside, making it more of a pleasant experience and, the sound of the birds chirping or the trees rustling in the wind, can become another base for you. When your mind does wander, (which is will because that's what the mind is supposed to do) then you can use these sounds to focus on to bring yourself back.

Along with this, if you choose to sit on the ground, over even lay, you will find more of a connection to the earth. This will help to root you can feel that divine connection to the planet.

Simple Tips:

· Turn off all electronics before and during your meditation

· Try not to meditate in the darkness as you may fall asleep

· Do all your chores before you meditate so that your mind is free

· Don't turn on the TV or check your phone right after meditation. Instead, enjoy how you are feeling

· Choose the same time every day to meditate and make it a priority

· Don't meditate whilst tired as you'll only fall asleep

Chapter 2: Breathing Correctly

We already spoke about breathing correctly and it's a good practice to try and breathe in a deep way while you meditate. Even if you don't get on with meditation, think of it as an exercise for the brain and make it something that you add to every day of your life. It's a little like thinking that breathing itself is necessary to life. The meditation process is merely an extension of that, in that all of your attention is placed upon the act of breathing and during meditation, you avoid thinking of other things. If thoughts come into your head, you don't make a big deal of it because this happens. Instead, what you are expected to do is simply acknowledge the thought and then let it go. Imagine the thought like a vignette or image that you pass on a traveling train and simply let the thought go in the same way as a passing scene would, adding no judgment to the thought at all. It's just a thought. It's not relevant to the meditation so you merely let it go.

To understand the breathing process, you need to be sitting on a hard chair with your feet flat on the floor. The important thing to think about is your posture. This is for several reasons, but the most important is that you have energy centers down your spine and when you sit in the right position, this opens these up and allows you to feel happier and healthier. Bad posture is really bad for the body and thus, sitting in the right position for meditation is important. For the moment, place your hands on your lap because I want you to practice the breathing method used for meditation and will ask you to move your hand up to your abdomen at a certain stage so you can feel the airflow and also the pivot of the stomach as you breathe. Breathe in through the nostrils and, as you do so, count to nine. Because this is more than you usually count when you are breathing, the air will fill your upper abdomen. Hold onto the breath for the count of three and then breathe out to the count of 11. You breathe out for longer than you breathe in as this helps to normalize the breath. Do it over and over and place your hand on your upper abdomen because you will feel the motion of your body while you breathe.

For meditation, you do the same thing, but you are always there in the breath, in the moment, so try to concentrate on the breathing even if you have to imagine the breath as a physical thing, going down into your body. It's quite easy to do after a while, but in your first attempts you will find that thoughts sneak into your head. The catchwords that you need to remember are "do not judge." Thus, no matter how bad the thoughts are or how distant they are from this moment, don't kick yourself for having thoughts. It's normal. Just look at the thought and acknowledge it and then imagine it like a passing scene from a train and let go of it. Go back to your breathing.

CHAPTER 3: BREAKING FREE FROM NEGATIVITY

Negative thoughts can be life draining. They can lead a person to doubt themselves and not act upon their dreams. For example, so many people get stuck on creating street protests but fail to come up with alternative solutions to the problem. While protesting on the streets is not a bad idea if you want to make others aware, it should be coupled with positive actions that can tap the interest of others.

Positive thinking is the ability to create and to inspire. It is not just about changing your thoughts but making sure that it translates to actions in your daily life otherwise the positive thoughts will not provide the impact that you would like to have.

To train yourself to have a better mindset, it would be best to learn how to calm your thoughts down. It gets easier to compose positive thoughts if your thoughts are arranged in such a manner that you can control them. Even when life gets too busy and hectic take the time to breathe slowly, relax and empty your thoughts through meditation.

Meditation is the art of not thinking about anything or just focusing on thinking about images that you would like to happen. The mind can be trained to see a much better perspective, for example, even a person in jail can get through the toughest days by learning to think positively, they can imagine the river banks, the sunlight, the forest and other desirable qualities of nature like roses instead of focusing on their plight.

In general, people do have the ability to stay focused, calm and can maintain positive thoughts. Encouraging others despite the circumstances is do-able. But to get to positive thinking, you need to learn to discipline your mind to overcome negativity.

Positive thinking is mostly about thinking about the present time and not worrying about the details of the past and the future. It is about training the mind and body to respond to what they can change now, not what they will not be able to work upon due to various circumstances. It is about being alert and making the most of a given situation.

The perception of an individual concerning things around them is very crucial because our ideas and conception of phenomenon influences our approach to things around us and our approach to things determine the result we get from the endeavor. Most of the time, there is no real difference between the A (distinction) student and the C (average) student, most of the time the difference between them is that one took his studies a little more serious than the other. Every great invention or achievement starts from the mind, i.e. everything good around us started off as a thought in someone's mind and vice versa.

It is important at this juncture that we recognize every person is a thinker and then there are two major types of thinkers! The positive thinkers are the first category of thinkers. They are the category of people that see the good in everything around them (optimist). They are always on the lookout to improve themselves and people around them. They are the class of people that see the half filled glass of water as half full rather than as half empty. The second categories of people are the negative thinkers. This category of people often regards themselves as realists, therefore they are easily de-motivated and often give up in the face of stress whereas a little burst of motivation could have seen them through. Negative thinkers take the easy way out of situations around them.

Comparing the two categories of thinkers, one thing is pertinent and that is the fact that it is easier to be a negative thinker than positive. For starters, it can be easily conditioned by parents unintentionally on the child. For example, a child that grew up with heavily critical parents will almost certainly grow up with little motivation about life. Also, in our everyday life, we are faced with situations that can be considered as discouraging to the average individual and although we can press on with optimism the average man will rather lose interest altogether.

It is important that we know that every one of us would have recorded higher success with our lives if we have been more optimistic with our thinking. Michael Faraday, the inventor of the light bulb failed repeatedly (reports say over a thousand times) in his quest to develop the light bulb but rather than give up his dream altogether and accept failure, he rather elected to reckon with the failure as simply a learning curve for him to do better in his attempt next time, and he eventually got the correct formula and today several decades after his death, his name is still being mentioned because he remained a positive thinker despite all odds.

Lots of students with great potentials have ended up mediocre because they doubted themselves, lots of sports stars, musicians and entrepreneurs have ended up small because of negative thinking, in fact, many great marriages have eventually ended up in divorce because the couple simply doubted their capacity to go the long mile.

If you have discovered that you tilt towards pessimism rather than optimism, if you are willing, you can make a transition or a defection from bad to good; the bad being the negative and the good being the positive thinking. *Here are 2 viable intervention steps to help you overcome pessimism.*

STEP 1: Identify the Negative thinking patterns

Once you replace negative thoughts with positive ones, you will start having positive results - Willie Nelson.

Let's face it, we are all humans, every one of us is susceptible to fear and doubt in our abilities. None of us is immune to negative thinking patterns but what we do with the negative thoughts is all that matters. It is expedient that we understand what leads to negative thoughts in the first place. The following texts details what goes on in the mind that leads to negative thoughts as well as the remedies to the causes of negative thoughts;

Filtering: In every activity or action we are faced with, there is always a positive side and a negative side to every activity of man but the pessimist will rather eliminate the positive aspect and magnify the negative aspect. As a result of the focus on the negative, there is lack of motivation to put in sufficient effort to get the good result that is due.

Personalizing: When things don't go according to plan, what do you think? Most people have come to constantly nurture negative emotions because they are fond of blaming themselves when things go wrong and because they are already used to self-blame their minds are already set on thinking negatively and expecting the worst of every situation.

Catastrophizing: This is an advanced stage of personalizing. Catastrophizing simply is when an individual due to past failures have now come to expect the worst in any given situation. For example, you support a sports team and you are already expecting them to lose even before the match begins.

Polarizing: Polarizing is an extremist way of thinking; the affected persons only perceive situations and happenings on the extreme. They don't see things in terms of success and failure, good or bad etc., therefore when they don't achieve the exact target they set for themselves, they consider themselves as having failed.

STEP 2: Pinpointing your Negative Thoughts

The following steps are helpful in overcoming your negative thoughts;

1. Write down the negative thoughts as they occur: When negative thoughts flood your mind concerning a future event or occurrence, endeavor to write them down.

This is very crucial in your quest to overcome negative emotion. If this is not done, negative emotions can eventually engender fear which will be inimical to the productivity of the individual. Write down the emotion and how it makes you feel.

2. Determine the source of the negative emotion: The negative emotions that you feel concerning an action or activity is there any noticeable trend in its occurrence? Is it in response to something or someone, or is it in relation to a past failure?

3. Determine how you react to the negative thought: The next step in your recovery is that you need to write down how you respond? Do you dwell on them? Do they metamorphose into catastrophizing? It is important that when negative thoughts come, you blank them out of the mind as soon as possible. They must be treated as an unwanted visitor and booted out as soon as possible.

These afore mentioned steps help to conceptualize the root of negative thoughts and sufficiently harm you in order to overcome it.

Chapter 4: The Gifts of Mindfulness

If you ask me, I would say mindfulness has brought gifts to mankind. These gifts are quite important to everyday living. It, in a way, detaches us from ourselves. It challenges our character and our reaction to situations, such as patience. Mindfulness is like cold, icy water thrown into a fiery furnace to enable the mind to see things more clearly.

Mindfulness enhances well being. And is this not the very reason of man's struggle? Happiness is elusive, yet by increasing your competence for mindfulness, you support many traits that contribute to a life of contentment. Being aware makes it simpler to savor the joys in life as they happen.

It aids you to become totally engaged in undertakings, and creates an increased capacity to manage adverse happenings. By focusing on the moment, many individuals who exercise mindfulness find that they are less susceptible to worry, detached of concerns about self-worth and accomplishments, and are better gifted to form meaningful connections with society.

And if that benefit is not enough for you, here is another one. Mindfulness advances physical condition. Scientists have revealed that mindfulness practices help advance physical condition through:

1.Easing gastrointestinal problems– Gastrointestinal difficulties is one of the many effects of stress. When stress is managed, a person experiences less triggering factors of gastrointestinal problems;

2.Assisting relief of stress–This is the usual result when a person detaches himself from events and making him not easily vulnerable emotionally;

3.Healing heart ailments–This is enhanced when stress and anxiety are dealt with properly or kept at the minimum preventing spiking of the heart rate;

4.Bettering sleep–Sleep is easier when there are less worries;

5.Lessening blood pressure - A relaxed state is necessary to control blood circulation in the body; and,

6.Bringing down chronic pain–This is especially true with some chronic pain which are psychosomatic in nature.

Best of all, mindfulness improves psychological health. Lately, psychotherapists have set sights on mindfulness meditation as an essential element in the healing of a number of dilemmas like:

1.Anxiety syndromes

2. Conflicts between couples

3. Depression

4. Eating maladies

5. Obsessive-compulsive conditions

6. Substance misuse

Some professionals have developed confidence that mindfulness functions partly by helping individuals accept their experiences, more especially those involving painful feeling, rather than responding to them with dislike and avoidance. Mindfulness meditation is also easily employed along with cognitive social therapy.

This improvement makes sense as both cognitive behavioral therapy and mindfulness meditation share the same goal of assisting people acquire perspective on contradictory, illogical and self-defeating point of views. Courtesy of HAMDOUCHI INTERACTIVE, LLC (COPYRIGHT©2011 MINDFULNESS AT THE CENTER. ALL RIGHTS RESERVED), here are some news features attesting to the gifts of mindfulness:

1. Mindfulness Practice Reduces Stress for Special Needs Parents

July 28, 2014 - This article in the New York Times describes how just six weeks of mindfulness training produced lower rates of stress, anxiety and depression in parents who are raising a child with developmental disabilities, genetic syndromes or psychiatric issues.

2. Mindfulness at Work Experts Discuss Its Value

March 13, 2014 - Meditation and mindfulness have made their way into the corporate world and find that mindfulness practice could be just the change we need in our busy, complex lives.

3. Mindfulness Benefits in Business News

February 12, 2014 - Forbes magazine highlights the work of Harvard's Ellen Langer on mindfulness, happiness and longevity. While the title includes the possibly misleading word "guarantees", the data are interesting!

4. Mindfulness Training Boosts Attention and Working Memory in Undergraduates

January 14, 2014 - In a study at the University of Miami, mindfulness training was found to significantly improve attention with no increase in the mind wandering seen in controls. As a result of the study, UM is implementing a campus-wide mindfulness initiative. A related study at the University of California, Santa Barbara, found not only decreased mind wandering, but also an increase in working memory and an increase in GRE test scores.

5. Healthier Gene Expression Seen with Mindfulness Meditation Practice

December 10, 2013 - Alterations in gene expression related to inflammation (the same genes that are the current targets of anti-inflammatory and analgesic or pain-relief drugs) were seen in associated with mindfulness meditation practice.

6. Meditation May Slow Progression to Alzheimer's

November 26, 2013 - Compared to the control group, those in the MBSR group had a significantly greater increase in functional connectivity between the regions of the brain most sensitive to mild cognitive impairment and Alzheimer's disease.

7. Mindfulness-Based Stress Reduction Helps Lower Blood Pressure, Study Finds

October 15, 2013–Blood pressure is effectively lowered by mindfulness-based stress reduction (MBSR) for patients with borderline high blood pressure or"pre-hypertension,"according to news research.

8. Physician Mindfulness and Health Care Quality

September 10, 2013 - A new multi-center study published today in the Annals of Family Medicine shows that physicians rated as more mindful have more patient-centered communication; part of a growing body of research supporting mindfulness training as a way to improve the health of both doctors and their patients.

9. Another Study with Teachers Points to Less Burnout and More Self-Compassion

August 30, 2013 - Researchers from the University of Wisconsin found that mindfulness practice helped lower stress, improve self-compassion and boost classroom organization among teachers.

10. Mindfulness Improves Reading Ability, Working Memory, and Task-Focus

March 26, 2013 - If you think your inability to concentrate is a hopeless condition, think again. Be in the body, breathe, and focus.

11. Mindfulness meditation may relieve chronic inflammation

January 16, 2013 - Even when compared to a rigorous control including expert teachers, exercise and group support, mindfulness, as learned in MBSR, is shown to benefit many illnesses associated with inflammation.

12. The Power of Concentration

December 15, 2012 - In this playful article on concentration, new research is shared on the brain and mindfulness practice.

13. Mindfulness Meditation Could Combat Loneliness In Elderly

July 29, 2012 - Study in adults aging 55-85 reveals that an 8-week MBSR course in mindfulness meditation decreased loneliness and improved inflammatory markers associated with heart disease, stroke and neurodegenerative diseases.

14. Mindfulness Reduces Anxiety/Depression in Those with Cancer

June 11, 2012 - No less than 35-40% of cancer patients suffer from significant anxiety and depression symptoms. Mindfulness-based therapy reduced anxiety and depression in a meta-analysis involving more than 1,400 patients living with cancer.

15. Teen Brain Benefits From Mindfulness Training

May 20, 2012 - Relationships and emotional intelligence benefits are seen when parents and teens practice mindfulness.

16. Journal of Academic Medicine article

April 27, 2012 - Mindfulness meditation practice in physician training encourages transparent and clear communication as well as better patient care.

17. Stressed During Cancer Treatment? Try Meditating

March 14, 2012 - Mindfulness practitioners and scientists alike are finding that mindfulness meditation as taught in MBSR can reduce distress and improve quality of life in those living with cancer.

18. Tired of Feeling Bad? Mindfulness and Emotional Resilience Scientifically & Experimentally Connected

February 20, 2012 - Behavioral neuroscience is finding that the more neurons that connect the prefrontal cortex and the amygdala in the brain, the more emotionally resilient one is; able to "bounce back" in the face of life's adversities or challenges. Mindfulness meditation strengthens these pathways of resilience.

19. MBSR Helps Breast Cancer Survivors

December 30, 2011 - MBSR can help breast cancer survivors improve their emotional and physical well being according to a new University of Missouri study

20. Cultivating your Plan B: Planning now can nurture creativity, ease anxiety

October 13, 2011 - In a world often characterized by the chaos of lay-offs, dashed hopes and "life unfolding," practicing mindfulness may be the best plan to ride the waves.

21. NPR audio: Rethinking Tinnitus: When The Ringing Won't Stop, Clear Your Mind

July 18, 2011 - Research with MBSR and tinnitus at UCSF's Medical Center reveals mindfulness meditation helps people separate the physical sensation of the ringing from all the anxiety, thoughts and emotions about the ringing.

22. The Wandering Mind and the Mindful Link to Happiness

June 26, 2011 - A study published in the journal Science revealed how distracted most of us are, and the price we pay for it. When subjects were paying full attention to what they were doing, they were more likely to report feeling happy. In fact, paying attention or not paying attention to what they were doing had more of an impact on reported happiness than what particular activity they were engaged in.

23. Lawyers Seeking Serenity Practice Mindfulness

May 11, 2011 - Charlie Halpern at University of California Boalt School of Law says, "It is making us more skilled and effective as lawyers, more focused, more active listeners, better at helping our clients and serving justice, and doing it in a way that is sustainable."

24. Mindfulness meditation improves connections in the brain

April 08, 2011 - Harvard Health publications reports on a new study, published in the May 2011 issue of Neuroimage, that adds to the growing data suggesting that one effect of mindfulness meditation is increased brain connectivity.

25. How Meditation May Change the Brain

January 28, 2011 - Researchers report that those who meditated for about 30 minutes a day for eight weeks had measurable changes in gray-matter in parts of the brain associated with memory, sense of self, empathy and stress.

26. Awake at the Wheel: Mindful Driving

December 10, 2010 - We often take our (and others) precious lives for granted on the road. There is science to support mindfulness as a valuable practice in all of life-- including driving!

27. To Reduce Pain (and Alter Your Brain), Try Meditation

November 18, 2010 - Study presented at the Society for Neuroscience this month shows meditation changes the way the brain processes pain signals.

28. Mindfulness meditation increases well-being in adolescent boys

September 02, 2010 - Mindfulness meditation Increase Well-being in Adolescent Boys: Researchers from the University of Cambridge analyzed 155 boys before and after a four-week crash course in mindfulness. After the trial period, the 14 and 15 year-old boys were found to have increased well being, including positive emotions such as happiness, contentment, interest and affection and functioning well.

As you can see from this, there is a lot more to mindfulness than immediately comes to mind and my approach of the subject was brought on by an event in my life which made me question my motive for living. Your approach may be something very individual or you may just be approaching mindfulness as an alternative to whatever your lifestyle offers you at the present time. The fact is that more and more people are finding that stress plays a large part in their lives and that mindfulness is able to tackle this.

Over the next couple of chapters, we will slowly walk you into the world of mindfulness because it is here that you will find solace in life and be able to let go of all of the negative aspects of your life, thus making it a richer world to be in. Does that mean bad things won't happen? Of course not – bad things happen to everyone – but what will change is the way that you perceive them and are able to handle them. Since stress is so prevalent in today's world, chances are that you have experienced more than your fair share of it and are looking for an alternative means of living that gives you something more than stress. Maybe you don't remember ever being happy. Perhaps you are questioning the validity of your life. Many people do, but have no worries. The answers that lie in mindfulness are all encompassing and will enrich your life beyond measure.

The quotations that I chose for this book are all related to mindfulness in their own way. The quotation that is shown below is no exception. It demonstrates that mindfulness is to be part and parcel of everything that you do. Remember walking through the park and going through angry thoughts because of something that happened at the office? The problem with this kind of thinking is that it adds negativity to your life. You are using the present moment – which should be devoted to enjoying the park you are in – in indulging in negative thought about a past event. Thus, that moment is wasted and can never be relived.

As you begin to learn more about mindfulness, you will begin to see how significant the quotation below is – everything that you do begins to take on purpose and as it does, you lose the sense of negativity that is holding you back – just as it was holding me back when my daughter became ill – and you begin to see that this moment really is the only one that counts and what you do with it defines your lifestyle and who you have become.

Chapter 5: Revitalizing Benefits of Mindfulness. Who Should Practice It?

Mindfulness has amazing proven therapeutic effects. However, this doesn't mean it cannot be practiced by people who are already satisfied with their lives and happy as a form of self-development. Since it can help you get more in tune with your deeper self, there's hardly any reason not to consider adopting it as a part of your life. It can be practiced by anyone regardless of age, of course. Still it is more imperative to seek solutions to a stressful life especially when you are older. Children and teenagers hardly have reasons to feel the burdens of life on their shoulders, don't they? In very particular cases e.g. if your kid suffers from ADHD, anxiety, or depression, apart from specialized treatment, you are absolutely welcome to try mindfulness as an additional way of improvement.

Now that we have outlined the overall positive effects of mindfulness that make it a highly recommendable practice, we should see when it is absolutely necessary to start integrating mindfulness in your routine. There are particular life situations when it is vitally important to resort to its multiple benefits:

• if you lead a rather stressful life through your profession or because of your family

 Mindfulness is going to help you relax and find relief, which will increase your performance at work and/or your harmonious relationships with your family members.

● if you find yourself experiencing difficulties when you have to concentrate on the task at hand

By practicing mindfulness you can learn to keep your mind in the present and avoid having your thoughts wander in the past or in the future. Thus, you don't allow yourself to be controlled by memories that should stay in the past instead of preventing you to enjoy the present moment.

● if you find it hard to set your life in order and decide what your priorities are

Mindfulness can help you organize your thoughts better as well as establish your own system of values in a conscious way and not simply go with the flow or let yourself be carried away by unimportant issues which eventually leave you unsatisfied on a deeper level.

- if you have health problems and you need to strengthen your body

It is a proven fact that mindfulness can lead to an immunity boost and help your body fight illness and cope with tension much better. Of course, if you are seriously ill, you should also follow treatment recommended by a specialist, but rest assured mindfulness can give you an extra weapon in combating illness.

- if you have to deal with emotional trauma or simply feel you cannot cope with the effects of traumatic experiences in your past

You may consider consulting a psychologist for solving such problems. However, adding this practice to your 'survival kit' will prove to be immensely beneficial, as mindfulness will help you purge your negative emotions and keep your painful memories where they belong, namely in the past. Practicing mindfulness is a great way of escaping toxic or tormenting thoughts as well as the tendency to relieve pain or to pine over spilt milk.

● if you have to cope with particularly stressful situations, if you suffer from depression, chronic fatigue, or you go through a mental breakdown

Mindfulness can help you reduce negative emotions and tension inside your brain. It is known to act almost as an anti-depressant. It can boost your mood and make you feel revitalized, ready to communicate with your friends or enjoy nature outside instead of letting yourself fall (back) into a black hole of sadness or get wound up by stress, worry etc.

● if you want to improve your general mental capacity

Mindfulness can help you increase your intellectual potential, your concentration power, and your memory. Try practicing mindfulness, it can be better than taking supplements such as ginko boloba or ginseng!

- if you feel you should have more emotional awareness and empathy in your life

Mindfulness can foster emotional intelligence and altruism or compassion in general. Through this subtle, but powerful effect it can act as a catalyst in your relationships, leading to notable improvement in your communication with people. It makes you more attuned to your own emotions and feelings; consequently you will also be able to understand others better without being self-absorbed once you are at peace with yourself.

- if you have problems when you have to regulate your attention on important things or if your are prone to procrastinating

Mindfulness can help you tune out distractions, even when you are not diagnosed with ADHD. Many of us may go through periods when we can't focus as well as we could. Maybe our brain needs to take a break and relax, maybe we feel dissatisfied with what we have and that makes us think about places where the grass is greener or dream of something different. Mindfulness can bring us back into our real world and teach us how to treasure the beauty we can find in every day in our environment. If you tend to procrastinate, mindfulness can help you connect with the task that you should do instead of, say, thinking too far ahead without doing something concrete.

● if you have a chaotic lifestyle, eating disorders, or irregular sleep patterns

Mindfulness will help you bring order into your life. Instead of overeating, you can practice mindfulness or simply savor the food you eat for its own unique taste in moderate quantities, not just eat to relieve stress.

● you feel unfulfilled, despondent, gloomy, or apathetic

The feeling of deep dissatisfaction with one's life may come in many forms, from brooding sadness to disappointment or mere indifference. If you don't feel happy and radiant, start practicing mindfulness. It will help you anchor yourself in your own image of who you want to be and it will gradually 'move' you towards that goal.

- last, but not least, practice mindfulness if you find yourself in a special complicated life stage or situation

Mindfulness is an amazing remedy for older persons, individuals who have to recover from illness, veterans, people who may suffer after the loss of someone dear, people who may be in prison etc. Essentially mindfulness is a great energizing and revitalizing solution for anyone.

Chapter 6: What Do We Really Need in Life?

We of course all need our basic necessities in life such as food, clothing, shelter, health accompanied with an education that can help us to succeed in this world today and hopefully live happy lives. Beyond the basics what things in life really deserve our attention and precious time and energy being used to accomplish them? There is a great old saying "Only the foolish go looking for happiness outside of themselves"- when we do that we have no control.

The wise saying continues, "Know that happiness and the causes of happiness are all present within us." So with the help of meditation we can learn to seek out the happiness that is deep within us not outside but inside is where the ultimate form of happiness lies.

Finding genuine happiness within. You could say that peace and contentment is the principal characteristic of genuine happiness. Your mind will become relaxed and at ease if you have contentment and inner peace as your basis.

When you are able to put your mind in a relaxed and eased state no matter what kind of crisis you may encounter in life you will not be disturbed. Your basic sense of well-being will not be altered or changed. You will be able to carry on your everyday life, work and other responsibilities much more efficiently and you will have the wisdom to decide what to do and what not to do. Life for you will become a much happier one.

You will even learn how to turn difficulties to your advantage. In order to make sure that our inner peace and stability are secure we must make sure to take care of our hearts and minds, as this is crucial in our overall health. Once you find peace of mind through meditation then both inner and outer harmony will soon follow.

Giving Your Mind a Job. Tibetan teacher "Mingyur Rinpoche" explains that when you meditate you are giving your mind a job- then once your mind becomes familiar with its job it will develop in the form of a natural and powerful transformation.

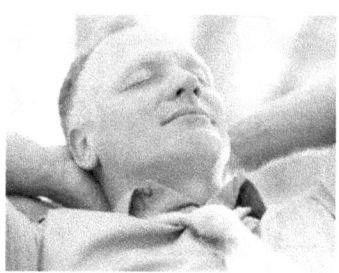

Time to Give Meditation a Try. First to get used to the experience of being in the present moment. Just sit for five minutes. Make sure to sit comfortably allowing your body to be still and breathe naturally.

Now let your thoughts come and go, try not to hold on to them or follow after them just let them come and go freely. Don't get great hopes of what you might achieve on your first session. Just enjoy the experience without too many expectations in play.

Five-minute Daily Session. Try to give yourself 5 minutes a day to try this form of meditation. Once you get more accustomed to sitting for 5 minutes a day to meditate you can eventually lengthen your sessions or do more than one session a day.

You must find a practice of meditation that suits you and your lifestyle. You could take notes after your meditation session of any insights you may have about your meditation practise.

Try and find a quiet and peaceful area to have your meditation session.

Meditation Experiences. Many people when first starting to meditate had found their thoughts seemed to be running wild from one thing to another more than they had ever experienced before. If this occurs it is a good sign. This shows you that you have become quieter and are now able to finally be in tune with your noisy thoughts and how loud they actually are.

It is said that at the beginning thoughts may seem to flow one after the other or on top of one another not unlike a steep mountain waterfall.

As you gradually perfect meditation your thoughts will become like deep water in a narrow gorge. Then they slowly change to a slow winding river making its way to the sea. Then your mind will become like a still and placid ocean only ruffled with the odd wave or ripple.

The fifth stage is that of stability which is compared to an oil lamp with a steady flame of light that is unmoved by the wind but remains bright and clear, nothing disturbing or unmoving it from providing a steady source of light within.

Meditation is not a quick fix but it is a gradual process towards inner enlightenment and peace.

Understanding Our Own Mind. Why is it important that we learn to understand how our own mind works? The real source of happiness and well-being lies within our minds that itself should be reason enough for us to want to comprehend how our mind works. You are not going to find real happiness in the forms that the outside world offers you.

If you don't find inner peace and happiness you will never be truly content and happy no matter how much "outer wealth" you accumulate without "inner wealth". You will always be a pauper in the sense that you lack "inner wealth." We have restless impatient minds that tend to be quick to judge with ideas of what we like, don't like, or things that we care nothing for at all.

Our thoughts are filled with what we do and don't like or things that we have fear or aversion towards. We are never content with what we do have but instead are constantly craving what we do not have and fear losing what we do have. As our minds become consumed with these thoughts we feel increasing levels of pain and excitement finding ourselves entangled in the endless cycle of dissatisfaction in our lives.

It seems that we basically spend half of our lives running and chasing after the things that we think will bring us happiness in life and running away from things that we do not want to experience or encounter. The Buddha refers to this as "dukkha" meaning suffering.

Chapter 7: Eight Meditation Techniques for Mindfulness

As you improve your mindfulness through breathing techniques, you can slowly add meditation techniques too into your daily life. Meditation has multiple benefits and some of them include:

Reduces impulsivity, worry, and anxiety

Reduces fear, stress, depression, and loneliness

Improves self-esteem and resilience to physical and mental pain

Improves energy levels and the functioning of your immune system

Increases focus and mental concentration

Improves creative thinking and cognitive skills

There are many ways of practicing meditation to achieve mindfulness. This chapter is dedicated to giving you eight proven meditation methods and if you implement them diligently you will have a sustained positive impact on your life. Starting from where I left off in the previous chapter:

Technique # 7 – Meditating by focusing your attention on one object – You should focus your attention on a single point or object. This could be in the form of a mantra, your breath, a visual object like an image, a point of light, or anything else that you are comfortable with. Allow your mind to focus on this object. This form is usually done with your eyes closed. As you advance, you will see your ability to focus on this object improve over time and the strength and depth of your attention will develop to powerful levels. You could choose from any one of the following or you could find your own:

Zen meditation

Kundalini meditation

Mantra meditation

Pranayama meditation

Technique # 8 – Meditation through open monitoring – Alternately, you could keep your eyes open and monitor everything that is going on around you without attachment or judgment. All internal thoughts, all external visual observations, all external sounds and smells; watch, see and notice everything but without responding or reacting to them. This kind of meditation involves monitoring all experiences without getting into them. Examples include vipassana and some forms of Taoist meditation.

Technique # 9 – Zen Meditation – Zen means "seated" in Japanese and hence this term means "seated meditation." The Japanese Zen has its origins in the Chinese Zen, which is traced back to the 6th-century Indian monk named Bodhidharma. Sit in a lotus position on a mat on the floor with legs crossed. Alternately, you could sit on a chair too. Keep your back erect, mouth closed, and eyes lowered such that your gaze is on the floor.

Once comfortably seated, you can either choose to focus on your breath or simply be in the present moment as much as possible. Every time your mind moves away, bring it gently back to either your breath or your present thoughts.

Technique # 10 – Vipassana Meditation – This is a conventional Buddhist practice. Sit on a cushion or mat on the floor. You sit cross-legged and keep your spine erect. You could sit on a chair but your back must not be supported. Now, focus on your breath. Notice how your abdomen rises and falls with each inhalation and exhalation.

Alternately, focus on the movement of air as it enters and leaves your nostrils. As you breathe, notice all other sensations and emotions going through your body and mind. Notice these sensations and emotions and focus back on your breathing. You must remember to focus on the breathing and take all other sounds, perceptions, and emotions as background noise to be only noticed but not responded to.

As you notice these sensations without attachment or judgment you will see that they are impermanent; they are unsatisfactory, and they are empty. Consequently, you will feel a sense of equanimity and calmness wash over you energizing you.

Technique # 11 – Mindfulness meditation by sitting quietly – This practice entails intentionally focusing on the present moment. You pay attention to all thoughts, all sensations, and all emotions that arise and accept them in a non-judgmental frame of mind. For a formal approach to this technique, sit on a chair or on a mat on the floor. You need to keep your back unsupported and erect. When you inhale, be conscious of your breathing in; when you exhale, be conscious of your breathing out.

Your mind will be pulled to other thoughts and sensations. Allow it to go there and then, gently pull it back to focus on this meditative exercise. Do not allow yourself to be lost in any of the sensations or thoughts that arise. Take notice of the thought and then focus back on the breathing. Be aware of the thought, but do not get into the thought.

Technique # 12 – Mindfulness meditation by paying attention to what you are doing – Even while you are engaged in your daily activities like walking, eating, or talking, you can practice the art of mindfulness meditation. Instead of going into an autopilot mode while doing your routine activities, begin to be aware of what you are doing.

For example, if you are talking, then pay attention to the words you use, the expressions on your face, the tone of your voice, the response from the person who is listening to you, etc. Don't let your mind wander off to some other thought.

Similarly, when you are eating, pay attention to the food, to the tastes, to the smells, to how you are chewing the food, etc. Chew slowly and mindfully. Finish the food in your mouth and only then reach out for the next bite. Avoid combining chewing and reaching out for the next bite simultaneously. Soon, you will eat find yourself eating just how much your body needs and rarely in excess.

When you are walking, feel your feet on the ground, pay attention to the moving body parts, pay attention to the sounds you are hearing as you walk, etc. The previous technique will help in your efforts to be mindful even when doing your daily activities. A combination of techniques 11 and 12 will add wholesomeness to the quality of your life.

Technique # 13 – Mantra meditation – A mantra is a word or syllable that is used to focus your mind on one thing. This mantra is not necessarily something that you use to convince yourself of some truth. It is just a form of crutch you use to focus your mind. However, there are mantras that claim to have specific vibration quality that enhances the power of concentration. It does not matter which type of mantra you use for this technique.

Sit erect and close your eyes. Repeat your chosen mantra silently during the whole meditation session. You could also whisper the mantra softly and lightly to facilitate concentration.

Technique # 14 – mindfulness activities – Practice at least for about 15 minutes each day any of the following methods to focus your mind on the present moment:

Use your opposite hand to do all the work – If you are right-handed then use your left hand to brush your teeth, to write, to brush your hair. Notice how focused you are on any activity that is not a habit. Soon you will be mindful of even routine and habitual activities.

Stack your books in a spiral form – This requires a lot of focus and attention and will help build your mindfulness attitude.

Adult coloring books – There are adult coloring books available in the market. Buy one of them and see how deeply focused your mind becomes as you assiduously fill colors into the intricate designs.

Mindfulness is the art of making the mundane sacred. The work you do is not a chore; it is a sacred thing that requires the full attention of your body and mind. When you slow down your dish washing chore and become mindful of the activity, you will feel the smell of the detergent; you will feel the warmth of the running water on your hands as your rinse; you will begin to appreciate the efforts of your hard work that converts a dirty utensil into a sparkling clean one!

CHAPTER 8: MOTIVATIONAL BOOKS AND SPEECHES

In the beginning of my third year I came across self help section articles on the internet. Motivational books and the techniques how to set up a goal and achieve them tremendously helped. I started feeling more energetic and enthusiastic. At the time I thought only motivation can help me. I would read and listen for hours the motivational books and speeches. In the crises when I stopped reading motivational articles I came to realize my energy level and enthusiasm significantly dropped down. So in the busy days as well I kept reading motivational quotes.

But I still dint felt peace inside. I had to constantly push myself to remain in high drive to reach towards my set up goals. I was very much impressed with the life of Bruce Lee and made him my role model. Beside his martial art, his philosophies attracted me most. His thoughts and philosophy hypnotized me and I worked much harder almost burnt myself. I remember in the morning when I use to jog I kept on reciting in my mind his quote ,"If you always put limits in whatever you do physically or anything else it will start spreading in your work, life and morality . There are no limits just plateaus and you must not stay there you must go beyond them, if it kills you it kills you. Man must constantly exceed his level". This thought would drive me nut and I would run until my lungs got exhausted. This practice started reflecting in my other work as well.

All the motivation helped me in the beginning days when they were new to me but soon the drive to reach towards the goal faded away. I tried to remain on the track but now the enthusiasm was lacking. Neither the good books nor the great quotes boosted my energy. Within short time my drive started fading away even when I spent hours reading inspirational books. Our mind can rationalize any thought very easily. It can deceive us in believing , this or that book will be the last book that will set me in tune . I thought I am not dependent on the books, but no, I couldn't put down the book even when it was worthless reading them. I had to figure out other ways.

To find peace and tranquility inside I switched to spiritual books . I am an atheist so Buddhism appealed me most . Also I felt he is more scientific and more psychological oriented.

LIMITS OF MOTOVATION

Motivation act as a catalyst to trigger you to get up and do some work . A true motivation comes from inside if you are dependent on outside stuff for your motivation then your enthusiasm soon will fade away. Motivation can be helpful to give you the kick start but don't get attach or you will end up in frustration. The rest of the journey has to be travelled by oneself . One should know when to drop the stuff . If you get too attach to it then you loose your path ,you loose your true identity by remaining just a mechanical slave to it .

Chapter 9: Who can benefit from mindfulness?

Now that we have discussed what mindfulness is, let's bring our attention to the kind of person who benefits from mindfulness. It seems the simple answer to this question is "mindfulness is for everyone," but that would be an insufficient explanation, so we are going into some details about who can practice mindfulness. Mindfulness is one of those practices that if a person does it, they find fairly quickly that doing things like quietly observing our surroundings or deep breathing brings some peace of mind. As such, it makes sense that a person who finds their mind in chaos is the kind of person who would benefit from a mindful practice. Mindfulness has been shown to help with problems ranging from depression to schizophrenia and everything in between. During my work as a research assistant in the ACT program, I heard examples of using mindful acceptance with schizophrenic patients, giving them the ability to accept the hallucinations that were out of their control otherwise, often leading to healthy coping. If mindfulness can have benefits to someone with schizophrenia, then they can absolutely have benefits for someone with anxiety and depression as well. Anxiety and depression are two of the most common problems that people seek help for in therapy. It would not be a stretch of the imagination to think that mindfulness plays a role in treating and helping people with these issues. When a person is chronically anxious, they tend to focus deeply on the concerns and worries of the future. A person who is chronically depressed is often plagued by memories of the past. With both of these extremes, it is in bringing them back to the present moment that they find peace. If you find that you are the kind of person who regularly thinks about what's going to happen next and worried about all the possibilities that could be, you can benefit from mindfulness. If you are a person who is very sad and hurt by all that has happened in the past, you too could benefit from mindfulness. If we acknowledge the present moment and look at the fact that we have no control over the future, we start to become more "planful" than worried and are more accepting of our past. Being planful is something that we can do in the present moment by looking at what we actually have control over, then doing that to help improve the future. Also, when we are in the present moment, we can choose not to repeat the past and instead we can make a conscious effort to choose to do new things differently. It must be noted that there are people who are not appropriate for mindfulness exercises because focusing on their thoughts can be unhealthy. People who have thought disorders or symptoms of psychosis, such as hallucinations, should be careful and consult a psychologist before starting a mindful practice. This is because people who struggle with these ailments can sometimes increase the severity of their symptoms due to the intense awareness of self and the internal experience fostered by mindfulness exercises. If this is the case, this does not mean you are less of a person or that you cannot overcome your problems. Rather, all this means is that you may need a different kind of assistance that mindfulness may not provide or a guide to help you practice it.

Mindfulness is a skill that you could use if you are in perfect physical health or paralyzed, it is a skill you use if you are young or old, and it is a skill you can use no matter what your religious beliefs are. Nothing needs to get in the way of you being able to practice mindfulness other than your own opinion of it. While it is true that sometimes is best to practice mindfulness in a certain way, such as in a quiet room or sitting down, this does not mean the person who cannot find a peaceful, quiet place or who cannot sit for very long can't do mindfulness either. If one finds there is a part of mindfulness they struggle with, it is possible that it can be altered or shaped to best fit your needs. As such, as mentioned above, the short answer to "who can benefit from mindfulness" is… Everyone.

Chapter 10: How to Practice Mindful Meditation

With all of its benefits, practicing mindful meditation is extremely easy. Let's go through the steps.

The Essentials

Wear comfortable clothing. You don't want to have your focus interrupted by a tight pair of pants or skirt. Find a comfortable seat. Ideally, it will be in a peaceful spot without clutter and noise. You can meditate indoors or outdoors.

Start your meditation with short sessions of around 10 minutes. This will make it easy to develop the habit of meditating and working your way up to half an hour or even a full hour.

Mornings or evenings are the best times, but any time you spend meditating works. You can also split your meditation sessions and do half when you get up and the second half before going to bed.

Getting Started With Mindful Meditation

Either sit in the traditional lotus position or simply relax in a comfortable chair, with your feet resting on the floor. Keep your spine straight but not stiff. Let your head hang naturally with a downward gaze.

Your hands should be resting comfortably on your thighs. You can keep your eyes open, but most people seem to prefer closing them. Do whatever works best for you. The goal is to get completely comfortable and not to worry about whether you are doing it right or wrong. Just do it, and you will enjoy the results.

Start focusing on your breathing. All your attention should be on how the air feels as you inhale deeply through your nose down to your stomach, then exhale. Notice the physical sensations of the air moving down your body, then being expelled through the nose. Become aware of the rise and fall in your chest as you inhale and exhale.

Don't worry if your attention wanders. This is perfectly normal. What is important is that you don't try to stop those intruding thoughts. Just let them flow through your mind non-judgmentally and return your focus to your breathing. If you find your thoughts

wandering too often, don't worry. Simply observe whatever is happening. Don't judge or blame yourself. Just observe what your mind is doing.

When you're done meditating, sit quietly for a moment before opening your eyes. Take a minute and observe what you are feeling. Again, it's important not to judge yourself. When you are ready, go about your day.

The act of focusing on your breath helps you become aware of your thoughts and emotions. The more you meditate, the more aware you become. And as we'll discuss in the next chapter, meditation is all about increasing your awareness.

Meditation Helps You Overcome Stressful Situation

Daily mindful meditation will help you cope with stress, but even normal days can make it challenging to remain in focus and mindful. Your boss wants to see you in his office NOW. Your spouse has been argumentative all week. Your child, who has just received his or her driver's license yesterday, has disappeared with your car and five best friends. It's stressful, and it's called life. Mindfulness can help you cope with these adversities.

Before seeing the boss, arguing with your spouse, or writing your heir out of the will, take a deep breath. Literally. Even if it's at your desk, sit quietly and spend two minutes inhaling and exhaling. However, you can do this exercise anywhere, such as in an elevator or while waiting for a street light to change. There's remarkable power in breathing. Just a few minutes will help calm you for whatever you need to face. These short breathing moments can be your own mini mental health spa.

You will also find that taking a mindful walk can greatly elevate your mood. All it takes is 10 or 15 minutes. You can do this outdoors or in the hallway of your office.

Walking Meditation

A walking meditation helps focus your scattered thoughts. It's a chance to work through the mental tsunami that can invariably ruin your day. You can do it anywhere, while walking to the store, to work, or through a park. Take care while crossing the street. When we walk in a normal fashion, we do so automatically, without awareness. We simply move forward from Point A to Point B. Not so with a walking meditation.

During walking meditation, keep your hands wherever they are most comfortable – at your side or in front of you. You may find it useful to mentally count out 10 steps at a time as you walk.

Instead of focusing on the rising and falling of your breath, you will focus on your feet as they rise and fall with each step. Be aware of your body as it shifts its weight as you walk.

As in a sitting meditation, thoughts will intrude. You will notice sights and sounds as you move. That's fine. Be aware of the intruding thoughts and gently shift your attention back to your feet. Another form of walking meditation is to focus on your environment instead of your body. As you walk, become aware of the sounds and smells around you. Notice colors and shapes. Don't

judge or react, simply remain aware. If your mind wanders, pull it back into focus.

Whether you do a regular half-hour meditation session at home or a mindful walking meditation on the way to the store, incorporating mindfulness into your day should become a natural part of your lifestyle. You deserve it.

Chapter 11: The Evolution of Self

People often go through their lives with very little thought about self. We are taught, as children, never to be selfish. Thus, it follows that often our thoughts are directed toward others or simply do not express the feelings that we have deep in our minds. I said in the opening that it is important that you have time alone and this is for a very specific purpose. If you are unhappy in your life, you do need to be aware of where that source of unhappiness lies and it's usually in the way that we perceive the world in relation to ourselves. You need to remember two golden rules when it comes to wishing for a different life:

You cannot control the thoughts and deeds of others and have no responsibility for it.

You can have anything that you want in your life, but you need to know what it is.

It's very easy to use negative things such as blame, retribution, jealousy, hate and all forms of negative thought to find someone other than ourselves to be accountable for the way that we feel. Unfortunately, those people we blame are probably totally unaware of what you feel and blame holds absolutely no purpose in your life. When you evaluate self, you need to take time alone, so put aside at least half an hour a day to think about what makes you the person that you are. It's all about you. It's not about others, so take these people out of the issues that you have.

Let me try and explain what happens when you attach your thoughts to other people. Jane was an unhappy adult. She looked at her life and discovered that the attitude of her mother made her feel unworthy and she had little self-esteem because of it. Her mother had criticized her life choices and had made Jane feel that she wasn't sufficiently intelligent to make wise choices. She was wrong. In all walks of life, we let people shape the way that we become and when you employ mindfulness, you get back to basics and learn who you really are and learn to love that person. So what do you do about all those people who make you feel small? The fact is that Jane and many people like her took up mindfulness and found that they actually liked themselves when they were able to put aside the opinions of others. When you are at your best, you will encourage positive interaction with others and will find that love and happiness will come to you. Only the desperate search for it and mindfulness helps you to replace that desperation with hope and fulfillment.

During the course of your life, you evolve according to your background, your education, your friends and influences and this evolution actually takes you away from the basic you. You may have forgotten there is a child inside who wants to be creative sometimes. You may have put these actions and activities out of your life and found that you rarely do anything that you enjoy anymore because you don't have time. Mindfulness teaches you all about time management because when you are mindful, you know that everything changes from one moment to the next and that however badly you feel in this moment, the next moment could totally transform you into a different person. Therefore, the emphasis is not on what could be, what has been or what other people want from you. The emphasis is on this moment, who you *ARE* right now and what you can do to make the person that you are a little better each day.

This applies to everyone. Even the perfectionist needs to learn how to be a better person and that may mean letting go of the notion that everything has to be perfect in the first place. We learn so much in life because we are constantly bombarded by noise of one kind or another. The TV shows us who we should imitate, but is that really necessary? Our job may cause us resentment but do you need to be in a job you resent? Your friends may use you, but are friends who constantly use you and give nothing back really an addition to your life.

To get back to basics, we need to write things down that we think describe the person we are right now in this moment and then go forward trying to correct things we don't like about ourselves and strengthen areas of weakness. Perhaps you are not compassionate enough. Perhaps you don't really know the meaning of the word spiritual and want to take things a step further than the surface to find out how spiritual you are and what you can gain from spirituality. Mindfulness helps you to do this and the silence that you give your mind during your mindfulness helps you to appreciate all of your senses and get back to the state where you trust your intuition a little more than you do now.

In a consumer rat race, it's very hard to distinguish what is real and what is supposition, but if you allow yourself that little bit of time each day for silence and then carry on through your day using mindfulness as your guide, you will find that you have a very different approach to life. You will become a better person. You will like yourself more and others will respond to you in a more positive way. You won't feel lonely. You will enjoy your own company and you will feel accomplished and happy inside which is extremely important if you want to go through your life in a way where you celebrate the seasons of your life, instead of dreading them.

Chapter 12: Understanding Stress and Anxiety and How Mindfulness Can Relieve the Two

Although stress and anxiety are often used interchangeably, the two terms are quite different. Let us first establish what the two terms are and how mindfulness can provide you relief from heightened stress and anxiety before discussing the ways to nurture mindfulness.

Difference between Stress and Anxiety

Stress is a natural response to danger or unexpected demand. For instance, when you are told to lead your team members in a project or when you decide to do bungee jumping with a friend, you experience a strong sensation in your body. This feeling of excitement and tension is stress.

This means that stress can be both good and bad, and whether it is good (eustress) or bad stress depends on the kind of stressor we encounter. If you encounter a situation that upsets you or places undue pressure on you, you experience negative stress, which is commonly referred to as stress. However, if you experience a demanding situation that seems exciting and enjoyable, you undergo positive stress or eustress.

Since positive stress makes you feel good, it does not bother you. However, the negative type of stress makes you feel frustrated, and upset, which is why it adversely affects your body, and mind especially if it lasts for a long time.

When you feel stressed, you also become anxious and apprehensive; thus, anxiety is one of the many effects of stress. While stress dissipates when the stressor goes away, anxiety persists even when there is nothing to be stressed about. Anxiety is a strong feeling of fear or apprehension that is mostly accompanied by unnecessary feelings of impending doom.

The moment your mind perceives a stressful or threatening situation, it triggers the stress response in your body, which is your body's natural way to handle the stressful situation. Your body undergoes a series of physiological changes triggered by the secretion of stress hormones such as cortisol and adrenaline. These physiological changes such as flow of blood to the muscles, increased heartbeat and rapid breathing give you the strength and ability to either fight the stressful situation or flee it.

When the stressful situation ends, your body calms down and returns to normal. This is true for serious life threatening situations such as being in a near-death experience, facing an accident or being chased by thugs. The stressful situations these days are mainly limited to being stuck in traffic jams, submitting projects on time, not meeting a deadline or having a heated discussion. Since these situations are demanding, our body goes into the fight or flight response while experiencing them and as we mostly have to endure these situations, our body stays in a constant state of stress. This means that the stress hormones stay in our body for a long time and keep wreaking havoc. This is why our stress turns into anxiety and we become apprehensive even when everything is calm.

When you are constantly anxious and stress, you experience the following problems:

· Headaches, body aches and digestion issues because the stress hormones directly and strongly affect your nervous and digestive system.

· You start feeling frustrated, which makes it difficult to think clearly. Naturally, when you are unable to think clearly, you find yourself acting rash and making hasty decisions that affect your life in general.

· When you fear things for no solid reason, you become insecure and this insecurity makes you uncertain of yourself and your capabilities. You start doubting yourself, which lowers your self-esteem and in turn your self-confidence.

· Heightened stress and anxiety severely and adversely affect your performance and when you undergo many slip-ups, you feel unsure of yourself, which further sabotages your self-belief. This makes it difficult for you to pursue the things you really want to.

· Being apprehensive and nervous often makes it difficult to be comfortable in social situations, which consequently affects your relationships and love life.

· Often, increased anxiety leads to depression.

To cap it, increased stress and anxiety make it extremely difficult to live a fulfilling and happy life. The great thing is that while these things are serious, you can still overcome them by cultivating a state of mindfulness. Let us learn more about mindfulness in the following chapter.

Chapter 13: Essential Foundations of your Practice

Like any endeavor, a meditation practice has to have strong foundations. Meditation itself is very simple. Essentially, it's just taking five to fifteen minutes in your day for some stillness, but keeping it up long term can be the challenge.

Having strong foundations for your practice is important to help you make it in the long haul. You have to turn meditation into more than just something you do. Other than simply being practical, meditation has to be meaningful and positively motivated to truly affect and manifest benefits.

In Buddhist tradition, meditation never stands alone. Attitude and intentions are just as important in meditation as mastering a certain meditative technique.

The Importance of Intention

The reasons behind why you meditate are just as important as the meditation practice itself. Your intentions dictate the strength of your motivation and commitment to your practice and it's important to have a clear idea of why you're interested in practicing meditation.

There are many specific reasons for you to practice meditation, but it often boils down to two points, finding peace and achieving happiness.

Getting in touch with the wisdom mind

According to Buddhist teachings, every person is of two minds, an ordinary mind and the wisdom mind. The ordinary mind comprises of all the racing, fragmented thoughts and negative emotions that pop into your head. It is the ordinary mind that desires control, and has an attachment to material things. It's the ordinary mind that is afraid of losing possessions, relationships or social status. Figuratively, imagine it as the outer layer of the mind, which means it is much closer to the consciousness.

The wisdom mind, on the other hand, is at the core of your concept of self. It is an aspect of pureness, even of divinity that is in every person. You're wisdom mind is always positive and hopeful, always full of love for all things and is always at peace. The wisdom mind is stamped with the character of humility, esteem and dignity. Your wisdom mind realizes its perfection, but it also recognizes this same perfection in everyone.

Your ordinary mind encloses your wisdom mind in messy, disjointed thoughts and emotions, making you unable to connect with your wisdom mind. It is only by stilling your ordinary mind that you can reconnect with your wisdom mind and realize your true nature and become truly at peace.

Improving life experiences

How you experience life has a big impact on whether you are happy or not. No matter how blessed life might be, if you view it through the lens of negativity and scarcity, there will always be a "reason" for unhappiness. On the other hand, when you choose to view your life through a lens of abundance and happiness, you can learn to be happy and at peace no matter what the circumstances are.

This isn't to say that when you are at peace, you become a passive by-stander. In fact, Buddhism believes in change and actively trying to achieve it. But it is only by actively changing and improving yourself as an individual can you affect changes to the world that is external to you. Meditation can help shape your way of thinking so that your experiences can become more positive.

Developing the Right Attitude

Your attitude can make the difference in whatever you do. In fact, your attitude could spell the difference between success and failure, which is why it's important to have the right kind of attitude. The only way you can get the most out of your meditation practice is by developing attitudes that complement your practice.

The Beginner's Mind

One of the most important attitudes to develop when it comes to mindfulness and meditation is one of unassuming openness also called the beginner's mind. The beginner's mind can be likened to that of a child's consciousness. Because there are no prior expectations, everything is new and wonderful to a child. They are curious and innocent to everything they see, which means they become more receptive to whatever arises.

Zen masters believe that meditation and enlightenment are not about acquiring knowledge and wisdom, but simply being able to maintain this innocent openness. You have to be able to incorporate a beginner's mind into your practice by clearing away all your expectations, biases and prejudices. When you go into meditation thinking it won't work, or if you expect that all your problems will immediately go away, then you're already clouding up your mind with unnecessary distractions.

Try to go into meditation with as few expectations and preconceptions as possible. After all, a beginner's mind is open to all things while an expert's mind is already too full for anything new.

A Heartful Attitude

Mindfulness and meditation are not just exercises of the mind, but of the heart as well. Everything you do during your practice must be infused with a heartful attitude. Heartfulness includes many other traits, but they all center around exercising loving-kindness towards all beings.

Heartfulness is all about relating to the world with love in your heart. This means you look upon others and yourself with attitudes that reflect your love.

Ø Patience – it is important to be patient when it comes to meditation. You can never really reach a meditative state if you are impatient with yourself. If you want something significant, meaningful, and transformative to grow out of your practice, you must have the patience to nurture it and watch it grow at its own pace.

Ø Welcoming – being able to welcome every thought, feeling and aspect of yourself is also very important. You must be able to welcome the good with the bad without prejudice. Simply accept your thoughts and emotions without judgment and let them pass through you with acceptance. Experience them without resistance, but with loving curiosity.

Ø Kindness and Compassion – one of the central thoughts in meditation is the desire to relieve others of pain and suffering. You don't want to cause others pain, so you choose to be kind; you feel sorrow over their pain and you are compassionate. During meditation, you should try to resonate with emotions centered on these.

Kindness and compassion aren't just directed to others as well. In fact, it is most important that you display kindness and compassion for yourself. You cannot spread love towards others without feeling love for yourself.

Being kind and compassionate doesn't only benefit others. Showing kindness to your fellow man, and even to lesser beings, gives you a big boost of happiness and sense of well-being.

Ø Non-attachment – according to the Zen masters, it is attachment that causes suffering, whether it's attachment to possessions, another person, social status etc. Consider this example, you believe that once you have the perfect girlfriend or boyfriend you will become the happiest person in the world.

If you don't find the right romantic partner, you can get depressed and frustrated. When you do find the "prefect" partner, you live in fear of one day losing them because they signify your happiness. Whether you get your wish or not, there is still a lot of stress and anxiety that comes with the attachment.

Similarly, if you get too attached to your image, you might end up obsessing over you weight or figure and get depressed if you don't achieve it. To practice non-attachment, you have to realize that your happiness is within you and you already have everything you need. One you get in touch with your wisdom mind, you will realize that you have every capacity to be happy and at peace within you.

Strengthening your Motivation

When it comes to developing a regular practice, it is important to have long-term commitment and self-discipline. When you start your practice, it is best if you make a full on commitment to your practice and set smaller, short-term goals that you can easily follow.

Short term goals to strengthen commitment

Don't center your goals on the results, but simply the experience. You can set a goal of spending 1 hour meditating on a work week and another hour meditating on the weekend. Don't expect that you'll be able to "master" meditation in a certain amount of time. Expectations can distract you and make you impatient regarding your progress.

Develop self-discipline

You can't expect that every day you'll be in the mood to meditate. Sometime you'll feel exhausted, sometimes you just won't feel like it. This is where self-discipline comes in. Discipline is about doing something even when you don't want to because you already made a commitment to it.

When you exercise self-discipline, you are not letting yourself be the slave of your moods or impulses. It can be difficult at first, but discipline is also a skill and you can get better at it the more you exercise. As you continue to make use of self-discipline, the less effort it eventually takes.

Chapter 14: Meditation Techniques

The different Meditations techniques are meant to suit all lifestyles and maximize the outcome. *Let us see the different meditation techniques so that you can know what options you have*

Mindful meditation

Here you need to become aware of your thoughts as they float through your mind but not dwelling on them. Research has shown that ignoring your thoughts may help you deal with stress thus helping you feel more relaxed. Actually, mindfulness is very useful in taming stress and helping in relaxation, and it helps you to zero in on thoughts that trigger stress and eliminate them from your thought process. The most effective way to achieve effective mindfulness is by choosing a quiet environment free from distraction. Take deep breaths as you concentrate on a specific idea for some time then, let the thought or idea drift from your mind and focus on the next thought.

As opposed to concentrated method of meditating where you focus on one specific thought for longer periods of time, here you think of different thoughts. Doing so encourages multiple ideas and increases the ability to be able to eliminate some items from your thought process.

Deep breathing

We all breathe but did you know that poor breathing techniques can result in stress and related disorders? That said, deep breathing could help you to relax the muscles, ease tension and stress while lowering blood sugar levels, factors that trigger high blood pressure. The key in deep breathing is to take a deep breath and slowly exhale and concentrate on your breathing as you exhale. Though this may seem boring at first, doing this will help take your mind off thoughts that normally trigger stress, anxiety, or depression. At the end of a deep breathing session, you will start to feel more relaxed as your muscles ease the stress and anxiety that cause fatigue and sadness. For your information, slow deep breathing has been known to develop a deep sense of wellbeing in person practicing this type of meditation.

Visual or object focus

As opposed to the mindfulness technique, here you focus your attention on an object of your choice such as anything that captures your attention. You may opt to concentrate on a flower or something else such as a neutral canvas painting that has alluring colors. Just like being mindful, this method of meditating requires a lot of practice as you have to be very mindful of distractions. However, when visualization meditation is practiced correctly, it results in very highly concentrated thinking. Actually, research has confirmed that it's very effective in stress management and relaxation.

In case you're running out of ideas, there are a many ways to visualize even without breaking a sweat for ideas. Try this, wash you your face and eyes with cold water, and then draw a black dot at eye level. Once done with this, stand about ten inches away from the mirror and concentrate on the present. As you do this, try and be in tune with your breathing and imagine that it is coming from the dot. Funny imagination but it's worth it, also visualize that the dot is also drawing its breath from you! In about ten or so minutes you should start feeling more relaxed and start feeling more in touch with your inner self.

Concentrative meditation

As the name suggests, concentrative meditation is whereby you focus on a single point or aspect, and concentrate on that aspect until when you feel relaxed and calmed down. Concentrative meditation may involve different activities such as sitting still, watching, and listening to your breath, concentrating on a single point or just a simple candle light. Sometimes you may opt to listen to a repetitive music or sounds like ocean waves in a bid to concentrate. Other people may seem to find repeating a certain mantra effective, where a mantra is just a calming word or phrase.

This technique of meditation requires you to be able to refocus you mind on your preferred choice of idea or object every time your thoughts wander off from the state of relaxation. Though this form of meditation is very effective in achieving concentration, it requires a lot of patience and dedication, but as you get used to a specific routine, it gets easier. As a beginner, it's advisable to experiment with different methods as much as is possible as one method may not work for you.

Creative meditation

This technique helps you to consciously empower certain aspects of your mind such as; joy, love, compassion, fearlessness, and humility. Creative meditation allows you to be more fully aware of your feelings and emotional states, especially in cases where you day dream. It helps you feel more alive as you are in tune with your emotions. It also helps you feel as if these qualities are more alive in you.

Creativity has been linked to day dreaming as both these aspects rely heavily on visualization, being able to transport yourself into places than where you are at that time. While you are "day dreaming" it is possible to attain a feeling of peace and inspiration, eventually, you will feel more inspired to continue with your previous task. If day dreaming, try to choose aspects that are inspirational. For instance, you can picture the blueness of the ocean water; imagine the wind on your hair or the taste of that Caribbean cocktail. If stressed, try to daydream on positive attributes until you find your stressing situation inferior compared to what you might have experienced before.

In creative meditation, when you are increasing your mind to factors like love, you become more aware of which factors in your life that bring about stress and anxiety. Doing so in the correct manner will help you focus on creating and assist you in strengthening virtues such as compassion. For instance, in case you've been feeling stressed over a promotion at work, creative meditation can help you develop patience and thus can wait longer without much emotional strain.

Transcendental meditation

Mantra meditation involves repeating your mantra by either making an audible noise or doing so silently. Simply put, a mantra is a repeated word or phrase that should help you remain focused and motivated. Here a mantra serves as an instrument of the mind that helps you get into the deepest state of meditation. Transcendental meditation helps in avoiding distracting thoughts and promotes a state of relaxed awareness whereby ordinary thinking is "transcended" and then replaced by a state of pure consciousness. When you are in this state, you are able to achieve perfect stillness, rest, order, complete absence of mental boundaries and stability.

To come up with a mantra, you can choose your preferred word, sound or a phrase, and repeat it silently multiple times until you achieve relaxation. For instance, you can choose words or phrases such as 'calm', 'peace' 'Om' or 'one'. Since a mantra should be effortlessly recited, ensure that you select a mantra that you can easily remember and automate. Be aware that you aren't restricted to a single or particular mantra so you have to feel free exploring your creativity. Then silently repeat the word or phrase that you like a couple of times when meditating. When you are at a "transcended" state, you are able to achieve perfect stillness, rest, and mental order.

With all the different meditation techniques, how do you choose the most suitable one?

How To Choose A Suitable Meditation Method

There are different types of meditation techniques that you may choose from. However, the final method you choose will be influenced greatly by your reason for meditating. Some people may start meditation for medical purposes while some may be doing it to achieve greater awareness. It is important that you choose a method that is best suited to your needs and lifestyle. You may have opted to use meditation as a stress coping mechanism or, you have decided to start meditating to achieve inner peace while in your meditative state.

If not sure which meditation technique is suited for you, use these guidelines to narrow down to your specific reason:

1. Set out a goal

Don't just meditate for the sake of it. It is good to be aware of what your end goal is; for instance are you meditating to achieve inner peace or, are you looking for a meditation style that is more creative in nature? The meditation technique you choose should be one that helps you achieve the goals you set. If your goal is to be more creative at work, it is advisable to use the creative meditation technique. On other occasions, it may be better to use the mindfulness technique in a bid to increase concentration. Just get a piece of paper or brainstorm a few goals that motivate you to meditate and you're good to go!

2. Choose a time

While some meditation techniques can be done during the day, some require that you set out particular times. For instance, yoga and body massage meditation methods may not be suitable for you in case you are very busy with work. It's a common problem to discover that you have less time in your daily schedule to go to a massage parlor or do yoga. If that is the case then, it would be easier to practice a technique that you can even do while at the office or while walking or standing at a busy street or bus stop. A meditation technique like deep breathing is quite effective if you are busy since you can practice deep breathing anywhere at any time.

3. Look for some inspiration

It is advisable to know your motivation for meditating before you start meditating. Actually, you may find that it is counterproductive to use a method best for creative meditation while you are practicing the concentrative method of meditation. But when inspired by something or someone, adopting a creative method shouldn't be a problem. In the creative method of meditation, you find that you are encouraged to look for inspiration from people who you desire to be like.

4. Relax your mind and body

It is vital for whichever meditation technique you choose, to be relaxed. Different people may adopt different methods of relaxation, and this depends on your preferences. You should ensure that you signal your body once ready to start meditating. Relaxation comes in many forms such as taking a relaxing bath before meditation and so on. Some people prefer listening to a specific song to help them relax while others eat a particular type of food that they feel helps make them relax.

Relaxation is very important. As you build your meditation routine and start with relaxing, you find that your body adapts well to that routine and helps it adjust your body accordingly. Resting gives you an inner peace, which is necessary for practicing meditation. Once relaxed, try to do any form of physical exercise to help you enter a deeper meditation state.

Chapter 15: The 'How' of Mindfulness

Of course one needs to be initiated into a formalized process of being mindful before they actually begin to discover the wonderful fact that they will become more and more mindful in due course of time without even consciously thinking about starting it. But if you are a novice where it comes to mindfulness, you will have to learn the ropes to get started.

Probably the best part about mindfulness mediation is the fact that it can be done just about anywhere – be it at home or even on the bus on the way to work. Outlined below are the top 10 ways in which you can incorporate mindfulness into your life, for the best possible results.

The top 10 methods of mindfulness meditation

#1 Sitting Meditation

We are going to be beginning with sitting meditation, because *sitting* is the first thing that comes to mind when one talks about meditation. This kind of meditation is for the conventional person; the one who likes to do things the traditional way.

All you have to do is sit upright in a quiet place with your spine erect. Close your eyes and focus your attention on your breathing as it comes into and then leaves your body. Thoughts and emotions will arise in your mind; simply observe them and then return your attention to your breathing.

#2 Body Scan Meditation

This one's a great kind of mindful meditation because it can be done in a chair wherever you are – in the office or at home.

What you need to do is to observe all the sensations that are coursing through your body, right from the air hitting your lungs to the sensations that come from the soles of your feet touching the floor. Feel your back against the chair and also the sensations in other parts of your body like your shoulders and stomach. Make sure you relax your body and be conscious of the way it feels in its entirety, before snapping out of your reverie. Thoughts and emotions will arise; observe them and return your attention to your bodily sensations.

#3 'Sound' Meditation

You can do this exactly in the way you do the other kinds of meditation discussed above – sitting on the floor or in a chair, albeit with a difference.

You need to simply focus on any sound that might be coming from inside or outside the room. Even if it's a quiet room, you will be aware of the sound of the fan if it is turned on and unless your room is absolutely soundproof, you won't be able to miss the sound of a horn blaring outside. Simply be aware of the sounds and if thoughts and feelings arise, observe them and then return to focusing your attention on those sounds.

#4 Walking Meditation

For the restless at heart, this one's a great type of meditation to incorporate into their frenetic lifestyle in order to soothe their frayed nerves.

What you need to do is find a place where you can walk uninterrupted for at least fifteen minutes – like say, in a park. Then you need to simply walk slowly

and consciously, and be aware of all the sensations that you are experiencing in the process.

You want to be aware of the heel of your feet touching the ground first before the front of your foot does, and the feeling of your leg rising in the air as you prepare to take the next step. You want to be aware of all the sensations in the other parts of your legs, such as your knees and hips as well. Feel the movement of your arms and the wind brushing past you as you walk. And yes, simply observe those thoughts and emotions but as always, return your attention to the sensations that walking process of yours entails.

#5 Shower meditation

Shower mediation- yes, meditating in the shower – can be one of the most effective methods of mindfulness meditation out there.

The best part about indulging in a shower meditation is the fact that you simply cannot come up with an excuse for not finding the time for it (you have to have a shower at least once a day, right?). How you are supposed to do it is really rather simple: you stand under the shower and feel the warm water course all over your body. Be aware of the sound of the water as it hits the

bathroom floor. Be most conscious of the lathering process and of the water washing away all the soap and shampoo from your body. You could even visualize the shower water as being rainwater, to give your shower meditation a uniquely refreshing twist. Of course you will find those thoughts and emotions come, but it will really be rather easy to let them go when you have something so relaxing and comforting as that hot shower to retreat back to.

#6 Eating meditation

You can eat your way towards a state of perfect mindfulness, by simply being mindful of what you eat. Let's take a look at how to employ this simple yet highly effective form of mindfulness meditation.

The first step is to begin by taking a good look at your food. Observe the various colors of the food in your plate and appreciate how aesthetically stimulating it might be. Then, pick up what you intend to eat and observe its texture. Bring it closer to your mouth and grab a whiff of its aroma. Then put it in your mouth and chew slowly and deliberately, completely savoring the flavors of the food you are eating. Finally, have a deep sense of gratitude that you are able to eat this food. You will find thoughts and emotions sauntering

into your mind like they are prone to do, but make sure you don't give them more attention than they deserve; simply observe them and then let them go, and continue you're your process of deliberate eating.

#7 Cleaning dishes meditation

You can employ mindful meditation most effectively when you are cleaning the dishes in your home.

All you need to do is to be completely aware of the fact that you are cleaning oils and other stains from the dishes, and ensure that every dish is thoroughly checked after cleaning it, before putting it in the drain board. You could tackle the dirtiest dishes first and end up with the relatively cleaner ones. Of course thoughts and emotions will constantly pour in but you have to make sure that you cleanse your mind as effectively as you do those dishes, by simply letting them pass through your mind without clinging on to them. So, when you do the dishes next, take the opportunity to make it worth your while – soon you might find that you are the one that opts to do the dishes every single time!

#8 Morning commute meditation

You can use the time you take to reach work, to indulge in a great form of meditation – the morning commute meditation. Here is how it works.

Whether you are on the bus or the subway, make it a point to observe the people all around you and also the view that you have of the outside. Make sure that you are well aware of the vibrations in your feet that are caused by the movement of the bus or train you find yourself in. There will be thoughts and emotions that will arise in you, and all you have to do is watch them before you let them go.

#9 Music meditation

We have already discussed how mindfulness can make us a whole lot more appreciative of music in general, but did you know that you could employ music itself to create a mindfulness meditation that packs a punch?

What you need to do is find a most soothing and calming track to listen to for a short period of time. Make sure you focus on the sensations and the sounds

of the music and dwell on the way the music makes you feel in the process. Thoughts and other feelings (those that are not related to the music) will arise, as they are wont to do; make sure you don't obsess over them and simply return to focusing on the music piece of your choice.

#10 Mindful yoga meditation

It's very easy to indulge in mindful meditation when you are practicing yoga.

All you have to do is be conscious of exactly how you are feeling whenever you are in any one of the several yoga *asanas* or positions you might be practicing. Let those thoughts and feelings come. Let them go and refocus your attention on the way you are feeling whilst in the pose.

Then, end with a sense of gratitude for having had the time to practice yoga.

Chapter 16: Why meditate?

About a month before i started writing this book, around March of 2014, I was settling down to play some cards with a group of friends when someone very close to me, an immediate family member, called me extremely upset. I'll keep her name private because she would be mortified to learn I told you all her story. She had just gotten into an argument with her boyfriend and was one the verge of a complete breakdown. They had only been together for a little over a month but she was clearly rattled to her core. Thinking that her reaction was far too great in relation to her argument with her boyfriend she reached out to me for help. Knowing that she suffers from PTSD brought on by some very serious childhood trauma, and immediately hearing the desperation in her voice, even over the phone, I excused myself and went to see her.

5 minutes later I arrived at her house she was standing over the sink in her Kitchen,

visibly trembling throughout her entire body, hyperventilating, and sobbing hard. After seeing me she tried to calm herself down but could not. Her mind would not let go of the idea that she was unloved, an old trigger from her difficult past. Every time she came close to the surfacing and calming herself her mind would reel with past memories, and current worries, and she would get dragged back down into a full blown PTSD attack. I could tell that she was present enough to understand that I was there with her and that I was there to help, but she was not present enough to let herself reason through her current situation. This, understand, is not her usual state of mind, nor is it something that happens through any fault of her own.

Sometimes life hands us something so terrible that the mind cannot handle it through the usual coping methods. When this happens the event/s can affect a person throughout their whole lives. This moment was her darkest moment in a long, long time. I knew what i had to do and I took action as fast as I could. I asked her to sit and focus on her breathing, breathing along with her to help steady her out. In the state she was in, her mind would reel like a bucking bull when she tried to turn her focus to her breathing. So I stayed there for close to an hour, serving as her focus, constantly reminding her to turn her attention to her breathing and to the current moment.

At first, her breath came in short bursts, but as she focused it slowed. At first, Her mind thought of the worst parts of her past, as she focused her mind turned to the present. Slowly, she came around and realized that the worst was over. We spent hours talking that night, and I believe the experience, while hard for her, helped her to see that the past doesn't have to control her. She patched things up with her boyfriend and has been doing very well ever since. I am truly glad that I was there to help her through this intensely difficult moment in her life.

More so, I am glad that I had taken the time to learn to meditate; I would not have had the tools to be able to help her regain control without the techniques that I learned through meditation.

As it turns out, there are a lot of reasons that these techniques work. In January of 2014, 47 separate studies were analyzed in *JAMA Internal Medicine* showing that meditation has benefits for people looking to manage anxiety, depression, and even pain. But that it did not help with issues like substance abuse, sleep, and weight.

So, why even bother to analyze all these studies? What does meditation actually do within our bodies? How are all of these benefits produced when all we are really doing is sitting still? The honest answer is that (in terms of scientific study) we aren't sure. The best answer out right now has to do with our Nervous system. Some researchers are hoping to learn more about the processes that are completed within the body that lead to such great differences when we practice meditation regularly.

The current prevailing theory suggests that meditation Works by affecting the parasympathetic nervous system regulations within each of us. It increases the activity in the parasympathetic Nervous system, and decreases activity in the sympathetic nervous system. For a quick look at what this really means The National Center for Complementary and Alternative Medicine Defines two sections of our nervous system as the following;

The sympathetic nervous system helps mobilize the body for action. When a person is under immediate stress, it produces the "fight-or-flight response": the heart rate and breathing rate go up and blood vessels narrow (restricting the flow of blood).

The parasympathetic nervous system causes the heart rate and breathing rate to slow down, the blood vessels to dilate(improving blood flow), and the flow of healthy digestive juices increases.

To anyone who has meditated for an extended period of time, it's clear that there are great benefits to meditation, Physically, Mentally, and spiritually. While we have some great ideas, we aren't sure what the exact biological cause is, but the effect is obvious. There is no downside to meditation, only great benefit.

Chapter 17: Meditation Technique for Beginner

The motivation behind why a great many people seek after the act of day by day contemplation is to mitigate their psyche and assemblage of the rigors of cutting edge life and ordinary anxiety. Individuals in these present day times need significant serenity and are looking for a feeling of clarity of things around them. With a specific end goal to stay away from the weights of the world weighing downward on them they hope to pick up this from interior instead of outer sources, for example, solution, TV or liquor.

There are exceptionally straightforward and simple reflection strategies for fledglings to learn without the time and cost of employing an individual yoga teacher. Most these just include basic activities, for example, centered breathing activities or listening to a compact disc while at home to guide you to a coveted reflective state. Once beat, one can then proceed onward to take in more propelled reflection strategies as they advance along their long lasting trip of contemplation.

Simple contemplation methods for apprentices:

Centered Breathing Exercises:

Considered one of the simpler contemplation strategies for amateurs who are beginning from the starting point. Numerous starting specialists accept strict contemplation position is essential, be that as it may it is endlessly over-evaluated. It is just critical that you are agreeable whether sitting in lotus, sitting easily in a seat, reclining or resting. With this activity, otherwise called pranayama, the specialist starts to inhale at an agreeable pace from the nose with eyes shut. Through a progression of timed breathe in and breathes out more than a brief time a reflective state can be come to with great core interest.

Guided Meditation:

Guided reflection is right now considered the most widely recognized of all contemplation procedures for amateurs because of its simplicity and adequacy. There are different styles and routines, however the guided bit of the contemplation is a reference to the aide you hear while you listen to a reflection disc. Regularly these album's will play extremely unwinding music, for example, hints of nature which help settle your psyche to set you up for reflection. The aide will identify with you and set the tone of reflection as they go promote into subtle element portraying different scenes and how to inhale as needs be. At long last, the aide will lead you into the coveted reflective state whether it is rest, objective accomplishment, association with your internal identity or some other reason.

As should be obvious these are simple contemplation procedures for apprentices to discover that go about as brilliant hopping off focuses to alleviate their regular anxiety. They help assemble a thoughtful establishment the same number of cutting edge reflection specialists concede despite everything they hone these strategies all the time.

Science has demonstrated that there are great deals of Meditation Techniques for Beginners in the same path there are a considerable measure of favorable circumstance that outcome from contemplation. Most think they would never figure out How to Meditate yet when they understand that Meditation for Beginners can prompt lessened stretch, wipe out and avert emotional instability, ailments and solution, they change their psyches and begin contemplating.

From an otherworldly perspective, the lines of correspondence in the middle of you and the all-inclusive personality is opened by reflection. So in the event that you need to figure out How to Meditate in light of the fact that you're after the physical and otherworldly advantages or on the grounds that you're charmed due to it, contemplation can truly be valuable to numerous.

Chapter 18: Meditation: The Most Fundamental Habit

It's no secret that I advocate meditation as a great way to start your day, deal with stress, live in the present and more.

But what many people don't realize is that meditation is perhaps the most important habit if you want to change other habits.

Be Mindful of Negative Thoughts

How do you learn to be mindful of your negative thoughts? Simple: you practice. And how do you practice mindfulness of your thoughts? By far the best method I've found is meditation.

Let's look at why meditation is so good for helping to change your habits, and how to form the meditation habit.

How Meditation Helps Habits

When we are unaware of our thoughts and urges, which arise in the back of our mind mostly unnoticed, they have a power over us. We are unable to change if these unbidden thoughts control us. But when we learn to observe them, we can then release their power over us.

Meditation is practice for observing those thoughts, for being more mindful of them throughout the day.

I will give you several examples in my own life, though actually there are dozens:

When I quit smoking, I would get an urge to take just one drag on a cigarette, and it would get so strong I had a hard time beating it. At the same time, I had these rationalizing thoughts: "It's OK to smoke just one — one cigarette doesn't hurt you", or "Why are you making yourself suffer like this? It's not worth it!" And those thoughts and urges would have beat me if I let them, but I watched them. I didn't act, I just watched. And the would rise and crest and then fade, and I would be OK.

When I started running, I wanted to stop when things got uncomfortable. But I learned that it was just a scared part of my mind that wanted to stop, a part of me that shied away from discomfort. I would watch that scared part of me, that makes me quit anything hard, and not let it control me.

When I write, I often get the urge to go do something else. When this urge goes unnoticed, I just act on it, and procrastinate. When I am mindful of this urge (and the accompanying rationalizations that come if I don't act on the urge), then I can pause and watch the urge and let it go, and return to the writing.

This same process helped me change my eating habits, run a marathon,change my clutter habits, and much more.

But none of that would have been possible if I didn't learn to watch, to be mindful of my urges and rationalizations and negative thoughts that told me I couldn't do it.

How did I learn to watch and be mindful? Meditation. It is the one habit where all you're doing is practicing this mindful observing, where everything else is stripped away in a beautiful simplicity that leaves just you and your thoughts and the present moment.

How to Form the Meditation Habit

It's pretty simple, but the doing is everything:

Commit to just 2 minutes a day. Start simply if you want the habit to stick. You can do it for 5 minutes if you feel good about it, but all you're committing to is 2 minutes each day. "Do Nothing 'Can You Do That'" chalenge at your Peace Starter Meditation app can help you and the sound of meditation timer is so pure, so serene and so perfect for enhancing your experience of meditation

Pick a time and trigger. Not an exact time of day, but a general time, like morning when you wake up, or during your lunch hour. The trigger should be something you already do regularly, like drink your first cup of coffee, brush your teeth, have lunch, or arrive home from work.

Find a quiet spot. Sometimes early morning is best, before others in your house might be awake and making lots of noise. Others might find a spot in a park or on the beach or some other soothing setting. It really doesn't matter where — as long as you can sit without being bothered for a few minutes. A few people walking by your park bench is fine.

Sit comfortably. Don't fuss too much about how you sit, what you wear, what you sit on, etc. I personally like to sit on a pillow on the floor, with my back leaning against a wall, because I'm very inflexible. Others who can sit cross-legged comfortably might do that instead. Still others can sit on a chair or couch if sitting on the floor is uncomfortable. Zen practitioners often use a zafu, a round cushion filled with kapok or buckwheat. Don't go out and buy one if you don't already have one. Any cushion or pillow will do, and some people can sit on a bare floor comfortably.

Focus on your breath. As you breathe in, follow your breath in through your nostrils, then into your throat, then into your lungs and belly. Sit straight, keep your eyes open but looking at the ground and with a soft focus. If you want to close your eyes, that's fine. As you breathe out, follow your breath out back into the world. If it helps, count … one breath in, two breath out, three breath in, four breath out … when you get to 10, start over. If you lose track, start over. If you find your mind wandering (and you will), just pay attention to your mind wandering, then bring it gently back to your breath. Repeat this process for the few minutes you meditate. You won't be very good at it at first, most likely, but you'll get better with practice.

And that's it. It's a very simple practice, but you want to do it for 2 minutes, every day, after the same trigger each day. Do this for a month and you'll have a daily meditation habit.

Chapter 19: Getting Started – Mindfulness Meditation

While the idea of looking inward to find a previously hidden well of tranquility and peace might sound either daunting or preposterous, the fact of the matter is that it is something that anyone can successfully master as long as they dedicate the time and mental energy required to ensure they practice being mindful each and every day.

In fact, one of the best things about mindfulness meditation is how very malleable it is, which means that you should be able to easily fit it into your schedule no matter what. When you are first getting started, however, you are going to want to set aside a set time and location each day to practice as this repetition will help you pick up the habit more easily overall. The location you pick should be one that is free of extraneous distractions so that you can focus completely on the task at hand. Being mindful is all about creating space between the information your body is providing you with and your reactions to that information. This means the fewer stimuli you have to work with at first, the easier the process will be overall.

Start off on the right foot

Make a commitment: Studies show that it takes about 30 days for a new habit to become a permanent part of your daily routine, which means you will need to practice mindfulness meditation every day for the first month for the best results. Unfortunately, for many people, this is easier said than done as mindfulness meditation is extremely low impact and requires very little preparation, making it easy to find an excuse to push it out of schedule – especially if said individual is already extremely busy.

If you find yourself constantly coming up with excuses to get out of practicing mindfulness meditation, keep the following ancient proverb in mind:

"Practice mindfulness meditation for fifteen minutes every day unless, of course, you are extremely busy in which case you should practice for thirty minutes instead". Don't let external forces dictate your path to personal improvement, create a meditation schedule that you can stick with every day and commit to the practice for 30 days. If feel like you are not seeing any results, at least you can say you gave it a fair chance. The odds are good, however, that you won't want to go back.

Focus on the moment: While your end goal should be to find a state of internal calm, regardless of what is going on in the world around you, it is difficult for most people to reach this state right away. Rather, they find it easier to start quieting their thoughts by focusing all of their attention on the signals that their bodies are relaying to them in the moment.

While, at first, you may not feel as though you are processing too much data from the world around you, especially if you are practicing in a quiet, calm space as suggested, this could not be further from the truth. The fact of the matter is that most of the time your brain filters out around 80 percent of the information it receives on any given day – which means that information is there: You just need to get in the habit of accessing it regularly.

Over time, you will learn to tune out the thoughts you have regarding your everyday routines, and instead tap directly into whatever it is that is going on around you. It is important to process the information that your senses are providing you while, at the same time, making a conscious effort to not pass judgement or dig too deeply into anything that crosses your mind. Judging results in additional thoughts in one way or another. And in turn, this creates even more thoughts. This accumulation of more and more thoughts will make it practically impossible for you to focus on the task at hand.

Remember, when it comes to mindfulness meditation the goal is to get as close to the moment as possible, which means ignoring everything else that is going on with the exception of what your senses are providing you. To reach this state, you will start by focusing on your breathing, especially on the way the air feels as it enters and exits your lungs. Also focus on the way the air smells and tastes.

Once you have narrowed your focus to only this band of information, the next thing you are going to want to do is to start expanding your observations to include the other sensations your body might be experiencing. With the top level of your mind temporarily cleared of your immediate thoughts, you can then focus on going deeper into yourself in search of the point where your mind is content not creating any new thoughts and simply exists in a relaxed, peaceful state.

Avoid your thoughts: When you first begin practicing mindfulness, it is perfectly natural for your mind to constantly fill with thoughts. This typically occurs because you have trained yourself over the years, whether you realize it or not, to constantly move from one thought to the next, in hopes of solving the latest major crisis. This is, of course, the polar opposite of what you are striving for with mindfulness – which is why it is only natural for you to expect a bit of an adjustment period.

When you find these types of thoughts breaching your quest for inner peace, it is important to avoid interacting with them and instead simply let them float away. Likewise, if you realize that you have started to interact with one of these thoughts, it is important that you let go of it without feeling angry with yourself for letting it slip in or feeling guilty for interacting with it. The fact of the matter is that any additional thought after the first does little good and only compounds the problem further.

While this can be a very difficult step for many people to master, it is important to remain stalwart in your convictions and avoid stray thoughts wherever you find them until it becomes second nature for you to do so. When it comes to clearing your mind as thoroughly as possible, you may find it helpful to visualize the thoughts that typically flow through your head as being incased in a bubble floating by. If you get trapped by one of the bubbles simply picture it popping or floating away to get yourself back on track. It seems silly but this is what personally helped me, so give it a try!

Keep it up: While early on in the process you may start to lose focus after a few minutes, it is important to keep pushing yourself to remain in a state of mindfulness for as long as possible each and every day. This is especially true if you find your mind wandering as you should be able to correct that habit the more you have to deal with it.

Trying to reach a state of mindfulness can be especially difficult if you have not yet reached an ideal, quiet state of mind. To understand the type of mindset you are striving to achieve, consider the period of blankness that you experience after you have been asked a question but before your mind registers a response. Finding a way to reach this type of state is key to your long-term success.

What happens next?

While there are plenty of proven positive side effects of practicing mindfulness, most of them are difficult to track on your own without specialized equipment as they occur at a biological level you can't see or occur on a mental level which is difficult to observe without bias. Instead, you will likely know that you are on the right track when you start to see changes in the mental conditioning you have been living with your entire life.

Modern society often instills in individuals a desire to hide their flaws and to treat any uncomfortable feelings or thoughts they have in much the same way. Over time, this leads to a desire to revise the truth and rewrite history, so it shows things in a more positive light overall.

Despite not being an especially healthy way to deal with existing issues, this common habit actually stems from the well-known flight or fight reflex that has helped humanity's ancestors survive against threats regardless if they were real or imagined.

This impulse helped your ancient ancestors survive, and even thrive, amongst the harsh conditions they lived with day to day. But these days, if this impulse is left unchecked, it can instead easily lead to a scenario where it undermines the qualities and traits that make you unique. This, in turn, leads to one of the greatest benefits of mindfulness: It provides those who practice it with a greater understanding of themselves, which is the first step to a greater acceptance of their strengths and weaknesses and the ways the two can be used together for the best results.

Regularly practicing mindfulness and sticking with it in the long-term can replace this negative mindset with one that is much more positive, which is referred to as radical acceptance. Simply put, radical acceptance allows you to more easily get in touch with the things you are experiencing or feeling in the moment, without having to worry about societal filters getting in the way.

Radical acceptance makes it easier for those who are deeply connected to past negative experiences to understand that the experience doesn't have to define them and has no bearing on the quality of a person they are as a whole. For those who are dealing with these types of issues, coming to this conclusion can be a truly freeing experience that is difficult to top.

A major part of mindfulness and radical acceptance is embracing the idea that all of your firsthand experiences happened the way they really did – and not in an idealized fashion. This kind of perspective leads to a greater overall tolerance for negative experiences as a whole, which should make it easier for these experiences to occur without damaging your mental state.

The improved mental state that comes along with learning to be more mindful also comes with the natural side effect of learning to be less judgmental, not just of your experiences but your thoughts as well. Cultivating a habit of remaining mindful means suspending your inner critic and take a more product look at your reactions, feeling, and thoughts and why they make you feel the way you do.

Finally, you should find that regularly practicing mindfulness will naturally improve your ability to be aware of what is going on around you at all times, even when you are preoccupied with problems or thoughts. Generally speaking, most people are so focused on the mistakes they have already made, or those they might make in the future, that they let the present pass them by without a second thought. This can be a difficult problem to avoid as it can be easy to miss the pleasures of the present without actually realizing what is going on.

Instead of existing in this mental twilight state, spending more time truly in the present will help you improve your total situational awareness which means you will have a better idea of what is going on around you at all times. This, in turn, allows you to more accurately measure your experiences to determine how they are affecting your sense of self without the baggage that such things typically carry around with them. Essentially, meta-awareness allows you to view yourself in a detached and objective manner which can benefit virtually every aspect of your life.

Chapter 20: Becoming more Creative

Aside from the other benefits I've already mentioned, there are some claims that the practise of mindful Meditation can help to help you become more creative.

Some say that it enhances what creative powers you have already but others disagree, suggesting that we all have abundant creativity and mindful meditation can help us to connect with it and learn to use it better in our various activities.

The theory is that mindfulness meditation helps us to focus on significant matters without being distracted by mental chatter to anything like the degree many people are.

This state gives us relaxation and greater focus. That helps us to consider each idea more thoroughly in less time, so we can process more ideas better.

When some research was done with a series of problems, the subjects who did not have experience of mindful meditation found the first few problems difficult and continued to treat the rest as equally hard. The subjects with mindful meditation experience looked at each problem as something on its own. So, they realized the later problems were much easier. That helped them to solve the whole set of problems more quickly and without feeling as much pressure.

The acknowledged benefit of less rigid thinking patterns is thought to maybe have benefits in the psychological area. Research is continuing.

But, it would be worthwhile for you to try some creative problems of a kind which you either like or need to deal with in your work before and after you have done some mindful meditation sessions and see if these benefits show in your direct experience.

What's the Difference with Mindfulness Meditation?

Traditional meditation is different in detail from mindfulness but they have much in common.

Mindfulness and meditation are often confused because the terms are used interchangeably by many teachers and writers and especially people who are selling products related to the topic.

For me, "meditation" is about exploring within ourselves and our connection to the world we inhabit. "Mindfulness" is about being aware. When we are mindful, we are focused on something we are doing.

The term "Mindfulness" is often used when promoting any kind of meditation when appealing to potential customers who have no personal or cultural connection to anything which involves meditation in any form.

My understanding is that regular meditation involves taking your mind off most of your current activities and concentrating on one thing which may involve listening to a sound or mentally following the passage of one breath from your nose down into your lungs and then back up and out of your mouth.

The effect of ***traditional meditation*** is to help us to relax by removing our attention from most outside influences to focus on a single action, sound or object.

This can be a tremendous help over time as we learn to block the other factors from our attention.
It will take time for us to get to the stage where we start to feel and understand the benefits of the sessions.
When we finish a session, we feel better and more benefits will become obvious over time.

But, it is a little hard for many people to become used to the discipline required to block out the emotional and physical pressures which are part of their daily existence, even for a few minutes.

It may also take time for you to be able to find a suitable place for your first few sessions where you won't be interrupted.

Some people may be put off from trying to learn to use meditation because of the historical association with Eastern religion. The Buddhists have been studying and using it for centuries but anyone can use the process whatever their beliefs.

Mindfulness meditation does not require stillness or isolation. You learn to focus on what you are doing at a particular moment and become more aware of all of the factors involved and how they relate to you.

This gives you greater focus on that activity but takes it away from external emotional factors such as worries and other distracting thoughts which may be unsettling or otherwise damaging to your concentration and effectiveness.

The mindfulness form of meditation is similar but we use something which you do or experience as part of your daily routine as the focus of the session.

You just arrange to remove other distractions where possible and ignore the others by applying more focus on the details of the specified task. You are not trying to block out everything, just giving something most of your attention for the time of the session.

You don't have to find an isolated place and you don't need to set up any special external conditions or equipment. No special clothing is needed either!

Starting to Learn Mindfulness Meditation

Don't worry about your progress, or lack of it, in the first few sessions. I expect that you may find the first few sessions don't give you much improvement, though some people do feel benefits fairly quickly.

It does not mean that you are not going to make progress or that you are doing anything wrong. It's common for people to respond to their first steps with any kind of meditation at different rates, just like you would expect if you took up a new sport or other type of activity.

When you read the steps to do your first meditation session, they are so simple that you may feel disappointed that you aren't pushing ahead.

But, the process is different to anything which you have done before and there are often physical and emotional factors which you need time to overcome so that you can get the full benefits of your meditation.

There are two other things I have learned about which can slow people's progress in their first few sessions.

We often focus on how it will feel when we succeed even before we have learned the steps well enough to make progress. This tendency can slow the improvement we get because successful meditation requires us to concentrate on what is happening at that moment.

When you were a small child on a trip in the family car, did you start asking, "Are we there yet?!" soon after you left home?

Your excitement is understandable but you don't enjoy the actual journey because you don't take notice of what is passing by because your attention is all on the far-off destination.

 Mindfulness meditation gets us to focus our full attention on what is happening at the moment, but that will take time to get right.

Another thing which some people do is to try to watch and judge how well their meditation is working. If we are following our breath from our nose down into our lungs and then up and out again, and we are also consciously trying to check if there's any effect on us from the exercise, at the same time we distort the process.

Chapter 22: Focused meditation

There is a very *clever guide* on focused meditation and how this contradicts to a certain extent the thought of mindfulness. Written by Bhante Gunaratana, the article explains the way that meditation on a set object is actually forced because the concentrated effect of that meditation isn't something that comes naturally.

The article further explains that there is a balance needed between being mindful and concentrating. If the balance is not correct, then the meditation session will not give the required results. If you let your mind choose the object that you will concentrate on, this helps because that's where mindfulness gets to choose what is fascinating enough to keep your attention focused on it. Some people use an object which is pinned on a string, a little like a Christmas decoration. It's a beautiful object which creates all different colors and catches the light. This helps the concentration levels while you are meditating and is not too busy to distract the mind from its purpose.

When you balance observation of that object with concentration, you center your thoughts and, in doing so, are able to enjoy the spiritual part of the exercise through observation and breathing techniques. Have you ever tried to focus your attention on one object for any length of time? Try it just out of curiosity. Something will always get in the way when you are not practised with mindful meditation, though when you are practised, you will find that this concentration is helpful to you and produces positive results.

Vipassana meditation is a kind of meditation that observes. In fact the word "Vipassana" means to see things as they actually are or to become aware of the status quo. This form of meditation is an ancient form, emanating from India and was used by Gotama Buddha. The use that it was put to is still something that is relevant today even though his use of the system dates back more than 2,500 years. The aim of this type of meditation is to get rid of negative or impure thought processes to liberate the mind so that it is free to take in more positive aspects of life.

People learning these techniques are asked to refrain from negative or self indulgent actions during their coursework since these have an impact on results. Students are then taught to concentrate on the breathing and to be aware of inhalation and breathing out through the nostrils. It sounds fairly basic, but don't be fooled by that. It's actually very hard to do properly. People tend to let thoughts get in the way of their practice because human beings are so accustomed to being too filled up with what is going on around them.

Once these techniques are learned, the student becomes much more relaxed and it is at this stage that they are taught to listen to their bodily messages and to gain control over the different messages that the body is giving to them, adjusting the way that they breathe or react to pain, thoughts, negative ideas etc. This helps a human being to become more aware and to reach a place of spirituality through bodily exercise to keep the body fit and mental exercise to keep the mind tuned into the moment.

The harmony of these systems of mindfulness is well worth achieving and students stay at the centers in India for up to nine weeks in order to improve their techniques. Many visitors from all over the world join these sessions to improve their mindfulness and their meditation methods.

Chapter 23: Mindfulness For Beginners: Everything You Need To Know

Being mindful means being aware of the present; it means being conscious of every tiny blessing bestowed upon you, along with everything taking place in the present moment, and fully living in the present instead of wasting your thoughts and time on the future or the past.

Digging Deeper into Mindfulness

Jon Kabat-Zinn, a renowned and brilliant mindfulness expert, describes mindfulness as an act of paying close attention to your present with deep intention and letting go of any judgment. He is a strong supporter of the belief that your present is the precise, real moment you have, and if you try understanding its importance, you will realize that your life does depend on the present.

To gain a deeper understanding of this, perform this little exercise. Close your eyes for a few seconds and purposefully avoid thinking of anything; merely let your thoughts wander and observe them.

What kinds of thoughts enter your mind on their own? Are they happy ones about your present, or are they sad thoughts regarding something you lost, or something upsetting you think will happen? If it is the latter, then clearly, your mind is deeply involved in the past or future, and is not aware of the present. However, if your thoughts contained an element of your present, then you may be aware of the present moment.

Be Conscious of Everything

When you are fully conscious of everything around you and everything about you, you understand that even though you did lose something, you have a lot more to be thankful of. Therefore, you start channeling your feelings of loss into gratitude, stress into compassion and anger into creativity. This brings you a sense of fulfillment and relaxation, which subsequently helps you feel better.

Let us throw some light on how mindfulness can help reduce stress, depression, and anxiety, and improve your mental and physical well-being. Doing this will motivate you to incorporate the practice into your life.

How Mindfulness Fights and Beats Depression

Studies show that the best way to become mindful is by meditating; the more you meditate, the more mindful you become. A study by Dr. Sara Lazar, a Harvard neuroscientist, revealed that those who were mindful, and meditated regularly, had a thick gray matter in their prefrontal cortex compared to those alien to meditation and mindfulness.

A thick grey matter meant that those who practiced mindfulness were in better control of their emotions and found it easy to manage depression. Being mindful is indeed a great and effective depression kicking practice you can use to kick the emotion out of your life.

Mindfulness Battles Stress and Anxiety

Scientific research has shown that two things prominently link to anxiety: low serotonin levels, and Beta brainwave frequency thinking. Serotonin is a neurotransmitter linked with boosting your mood; the better its levels are in the body/brain, the better your mood will be.

Beta brainwave is one of the five brainwaves. The frequency of each brainwave pattern brings different changes in your thinking and behavior. Beta brainwave is a high frequency brainwave activated when you experience stress. When your serotonin levels are low, and your brainwave pattern falls in the Beta region, you start experiencing stress and gradually become highly anxious.

To combat anxiety issues, you need to manage these factors; mindfulness can easily help with these tasks. Mindfulness helps you become calm, which consequently improves serotonin levels in your brain, helping you become happier and less anxious. Moreover, mindfulness relaxes your brainwaves thus helping them enter the Theta brainwave frequency, a low-frequency brainwave that makes you feel peaceful and calm. Therefore, by practicing mindfulness regularly, you can successfully treat anxiety and most brain and mood related conditions.

Mindfulness Improves Emotional Well-being

The moment you successfully tackle depression, stress and anxiety, your mental well-being automatically improves. There is no doubt in the fact that mindfulness improves your emotional well-being.

Moreover, mindfulness helps you realize all the pleasures of life you had been missing by creating awareness of the gifts your life has showered upon you. This makes you appreciate these blessings thus providing you with a sense of fulfillment, which in turn boosts your serotonin levels and makes you feel happy.

In addition, mindfulness makes it easy for you to savor different pleasures in life, which helps you become engaged in routine activities. This helps you enjoy each moment as it comes and live it to the fullest. In addition, mindfulness improves your capacity to deal with adversities and emerge victorious even when the going gets tough.

When you focus on what is here right now, you are less likely to engage in different concerns regarding your future, or any regrets pertinent to the past; you become less pensive about concerns regarding self-esteem and success, and are able to form deeper and better connections with others. This improves your relationships with loved ones, thus improving your emotional well-being even more.

Mindfulness Enhances Physical Well-being

Scientists have proven that mindfulness can provide you relief from blood pressure issues, chronic pains, insomnia, heart conditions, and gastrointestinal difficulties. Moreover, mindfulness effectively helps you combat conditions such as substance abuse, eating disorders, depression, anxiety disorders, and obsessive-compulsive disorders. When these problems vacate your life, your health starts improving.

As stated above, mindfulness enhances your emotional well-being; when your mind relaxes and your emotions are balance, you start focusing on yourself and begin paying attention to your body, which consequently improves your physical well-being.

To sum it up, mindfulness is a magnificent technique that can help improve every aspect of your life including social, physical, mental, relationship, career, and personal. By making room for mindfulness in your life, you can easily infuse harmony and happiness in your life.

Chapter 24: Group Mindfulness and More Tips

Being aware and mindful means becoming friends with the present moment and all that your own experience entails, including your own feelings, perceptions, thoughts, and bodily sensations. This should be approached with an attitude of acceptance, curiosity, and openness. Mindfulness connects you to the moment and frees you from the tyranny of your own mind, and most of us need more of that in our lives.

Mindfulness Method Number Nine: Make it a Group Effort.

Humans are social creatures, meaning that we benefit from being involved with others and draw inspiration and motivation from that. Find at least one friend who would like to join in on your mindfulness practice, or see if you can find a meditation circle to join in your area. If you do not have access to this, make it a more social activity by dedicating your mindfulness or meditation to those in need across the world.

Mindfulness Method Number Ten: Always Stay Disciplined.

In your mindfulness practice, make sure that your daily routine is highly structured. Meditate each day at the same place and time. You should also strictly adhere to the instructions you have set for yourself about posture, breath, and where you place your hands.

More Tips to Help you with Mindfulness:

In addition to the 1o methods given to you in this book, there are a few other tips you can follow to ensure that you stay on the right track with your mindfulness practice. Each and every day, follow these tips, whether you are at home, on your day off, working, or in a social setting:

Learn to Be Instead of to Do: Most of us have a compulsion to fill every hour of our days with activity, but resist this and instead give yourself permission to simply exist and enjoy the moment. As soon as your mind begins to wander, gently remind yourself of your intention to clear your mind and be present in the current moment.

Your Thoughts are Thoughts: Perhaps the most central aspect of mindfulness is realizing that your thoughts are only thoughts and cannot harm you unless you react to or believe in them instantly.

Pay Attention: When do you tend to lose focus and space out? Is it during class, or while brushing your teeth? This is the activity you need to focus on being more mindful toward.

Get better at Listening: Listening is a highly mindful activity. This includes both listening to others and to yourself. Practice paying close attention when others talk instead of just waiting for your turn to speak like most people do. This helps you remember to stay mindful instead of getting lost in distraction.

Be Outside More: It is much easier to be conscious when you are outside in nature because it is so calm and still. Make sure that you are going outside to walk at least once a day and this will help you remain more mindful.

Chapter 25: What is Mindfulness?

There is no easy answer to this question. It is very hard or near to impossible to relive experiences or emotions through words. What the experience of mindfulness might mean to one person will not necessarily be the same as the other person. Everyone is different and so their reaction to similar practices are also different.

However if a forced effort was to be made then mindfulness can be equated with a sense of heightened awareness. This synonymy should be considered with caution though.

Everything that exists in this universe is a part of a big circle of life. In other words it is all connected to each other. The plants, the animals, the sun, the stars, the clouds are all a part of one big system. Mindfulness means being aware of this connection at all times throughout our existence.

At this stage, this might sound confusing. To simplify it, take it this way that the whole universe is like a body and this body is inhibited by a soul. Some believe this soul of the universe to be God, Higher Power, Higher Energy or even Probability and Randomness. The discussion about the soul of the universe is beyond the scope of this book. What concerns us is that we all are a part of the body of the universe. The animals, plants, sun, moon and stars are all tiny organs in the body of the universe.

Now that we have established that, pause for a moment and consider your own body. You are in sync with so many of its functions. You are unconsciously sentient that you're breathing, your heart is beating, your eyes are moving as you read this. All of this is happening at the same time and you are aware of it. Similarly mindfulness means being aware of the body of the universe of which we are a part.

Often times, when we are walking down a road or strolling through the park, we are not connected with the events around us. We are so absorbed in our own thoughts and plans that we tend to ignore all that is happening around us. The winds blowing through our hair, the crunch of leaves beneath our feet, the golden sunshine on our faces; we are oblivious to all the beauty around us.

It is a common occurrence that when you get home from a walk around the block, you cannot recall all the details of your stroll. You can at maximum pin point a few landmarks or any unusual occurrences that might have taken place. The rest, you tend to ignore as being too mundane.

Why is it that we are so hell bent on remembering and taking note of only the extraordinary? When most of our lives pass amongst the things that we categorize as mundane. Why do we so consciously chose to not enrich our experience with everyday happenings?

In this context, a young child is much better than us. She/he is much more mindful of the happenings around her/him. Everything to her/him is a small wonder and a miracle to be appreciated and to be overjoyed about. Adults can learn mindfulness from a child. She/he has nowhere to go, nowhere to be and most importantly no role to play. She/he is perfectly content being where she/he is with whatever she/he has.

In a sense, being mindful of everything around us negates our ego. We are actively making the decision that the world around us, the body of the universe is much more important than the endless stream of thoughts inside our heads. We are realizing that what the universe is trying to tell us is more significant than what we are trying to tell ourselves. Rising above our egos and self-importance is perhaps the most vital part of mindfulness. When we decide to leave ourselves behind is when we begin the process of unification with the universe.

At some point in our lives, we all have experienced the calm that comes with being perfectly mindful. For most of us, such experiences are associated with religious practices. In prayer and supplication. In chanting slogans and rhymes. In staring at idols and symbols. In places where God is supposed to dwell.

This is so because we have been taught to believe that in the presence of God or the word of God, all other worldly thoughts should be banished. We actively concentrate on being fully present there. It is this active concentration to "be" that is mindfulness. In that moment of active concentration, we are fully aware of all that is happening in the body of the universe. We are aware of the earth beneath our feet and the roof above our heads. In those moments our minds and bodies are both in the present. We achieve unity within ourselves hence we become one with the world.

Imagine if we could exercise this presence of mind throughout our lives. How much more enriched and complete our existence would be. How much of our self-created troubles would vanish if we just chose to keep our mind and bodies in sync. Instead we choose to pay heed to our egos and our small selves and in the bargain exchange our peace of mind for a despondent existence.

Conclusion

This has been a short book, but I hope that it's enough to make you enthusiastic about learning to use mindfulness in your life. If you feel that you are not capable of meditating without instruction, by all means join a class and mix with others who are trying to find that happiness that is held in a moment of mindfulness.

You will find that your life will change considerably, that you will be happier and that you will be more capable of seeing other person's viewpoint when you practice mindfulness on an ongoing basis. Enjoy your food and the tastes and aromas of the food that you eat. You will find that mindful people tend to know what's good for their bodies and listen to what their bodies have to say. You will know when you have experienced something wonderful. I remember the first time that I ever ate a fig fresh from the tree. I remember when I played my first note on a guitar correctly. Every experience that you are given in this life should be used to positively reinforce that you enjoyed the moment that you were in and appreciated the strength that you gained from adversity.

Even though life may throw bricks sometimes, what this does is give you the strength to get through those moments that are difficult and to be strong enough to be able to face them. Then, strengthened by your belief in life and in the moment, you will be able to pass from adversity into a new moment and a new opportunity to find happiness and contentment.

www.ingramcontent.com/pod-product-compliance
Lightning Source LLC
Chambersburg PA
CBHW072013070526
44583CB00015B/1468